D1236364

IN SEARCH OF TALMUDIC BIOGRAPHY

Program in Judaic Studies
Brown University
BROWN JUDAIC STUDIES
Edited by
Jacob Neusner,
Wendell S. Dietrich, Ernest S. Frerichs,
Alan Zuckerman

Project Editors (Project)

David Blumenthal, Emory University (Approaches to Medieval Judaism)
Ernest S. Frerichs, Brown University (Dissertations and Monographs)
Lenn Evan Goodman, University of Hawaii (Studies in Medieval Judaism)
William Scott Green, University of Rochester (Approaches to Ancient Judaism)
Ivan Marcus, Jewish Theological Seminary of Americas
(Texts and Studies in Medieval Judaism)
Marc L. Raphael, Ohio State University (Approaches to Judaism in Modern Times)
Jonathan Z. Smith, University of Chicago (Studia Philonica)

Number 70
IN SEARCH OF TALMUDIC BIOGRAPHY
The Problem of the Attributed Saying

by
Jacob Neusner

IN SEARCH OF TALMUDIC BIOGRAPHY
The Problem of the Attributed Saying

by
Jacob Neusner

Scholars Press
Chico, California

IN SEARCH OF TALMUDIC BIOGRAPHY
The Problem of the Attributed Saying

by
Jacob Neusner

BM
502.3
.E4
N49
1984

Library of Congress Cataloging in Publication Data

Neusner, Jacob, 1932–
  In search of Talmudic biography.

  (Brown Judaic studies ; no. 70)
  Bibliography: p.
  Includes index.
  1. Eliezer ben Hyrcanus. 2. Tannaim—Biography.
3. Rabbinical literature—History and criticism.
I. Title. II. Series
BM502.3.E4N49 1984 296.1'206   84–10526
ISBN 0-89130-752-4

Printed in the United States of America

For

LOUIS H. FELDMAN

on the occasion of

the appearance of his magisterial work

Josephus and Modern Scholarship

A salute to the scholar and a

gesture of thanks to the friend

CONTENTS

PREFACE

This is a book about how biography figures in a literature that pays little attention to "lives" and contains no sustained biography. What I wish to do is trace how, in the literature at hand, individuals -- exemplified by one man -- play their distinctive role and contribute to the formation of a collective and common canon. In the pages that follow I take seriously the ubiquitous claim of editors and redactors that named individuals said and did certain things and to ask about the formation of convictions and the transmission of traditions about what named individuals said and did. That is, how do we get as much "biography" as the canon at hand contains. In the end we confront an astonishing paradox, namely, a literature that speaks authoritatively for all, yet bears numerous named passages, assigned to the minority of one, who is named. We take up a collection of documents that speak in a single and uniform voice and yet claim to tell us what numerous dissenters had to say. We turn to writings rich in biographical materials yet presented anonymously, and we review private opinions claiming normative status, that is, sayings and stories imputed to individuals, preserved in writings denying that individuals matter. Just what does the literature at hand propose to say in the name of, and about, individuals? where and how do they speak? and what role is reserved for the one among the many? -- That is the set of questions I answer here.

The canon of sacred writings under study derives from sages of Judaism, called rabbis as an honorific title, who lived from the late first century through the sixth. They produced systematic exegesis of two basic books, the Hebrew Scriptures known to the world as the Old Testament, and the Mishnah, a philosophical law code closed at ca. A.D. 200. Their commentaries on the former express rabbis' ideas in the setting of exegesis of verses of some biblical books; their commentaries on the latter, called Talmuds (of which there were two, one produced in the Land of Israel, the other in Babylonia), contain rabbis' ideas in the context of exegesis of sentences of tractates of the Mishnah. Rabbis certainly produced some of the translations of Scripture into Aramaic, and they may stand behind the formation of the liturgy of Judaism we have in the Siddur and Mahzor (though hardly in the forms in which those books now exist). But their principal and paramount literary heritage is contained within the exegesis of the Scriptures and the Mishnah.

That fact is important and bears restatement in the context of the problem before us.

While rabbinic literature encompasses brief compositions of diverse types, when reaching redaction, these types take only two forms: commentaries to the Mishnah and secondary expansions thereof, commentaries to Scripture and generalizations and encompassing propositions resting thereon. This is important to the study of ancient lives, because in neither type of redactional work do stories about individuals find a natural

- 1 -

place. Why not? Exegesis of the Mishnah and of Scripture alike may reach full expression without appeal to the character and personality of the exegete or of authorities that are cited. Among the forms and types of rabbinic compositions, from the Mishnah at ca. A.D. 200 through the Talmud of Babylonia at ca. A.D. 600, with a broad and sizable corpus of writings in between, we find none centered upon an individual. There is no collection, for example, of sayings attributed to a given person. There is no composition of tales and stories into a sustained biography.

Where rabbis do appear, moreover, tales serve to present the rabbi not as an individual and a hero, but as a model and an exemplar of collective values, collectively framed, uniformly embodied. Since these facts strongly suggest that within the imaginative and creative life of the formative minds of Judaism people found little place for biography, let alone use and purpose for the processes of individuation and characterization (whether imaginary or historical hardly matters), we must then wonder at a simple paradoxical and fact. It is that the rabbinic literature is built out of sayings attributed to individuals, and stories told about them. So the literary character of the movement contradicts the essential quality of the documents. Books without named authors, speaking in general terms about what everyone should do and strive to become, feature individuals' words and deeds, which, by definition, speak for one person at a time, though (self-evidently) merging with the collectivity that, in sum, we call Judaism.

In this book I propose to trace the formation of the record of an individual in a social world that provided no place for biography and in a religious movement that aimed at imparting the same, shared traits to everyone. Let me now expand upon what is at hand.

The form of Judaism documented by the Mishnah, two Talmuds, compilations of exegetical comments on Scripture ("midrashim"), and related writings produced no biographies. But that form of Judaism bears the name of its authority-figure, the rabbi, or of its the principal document of that same figure, the Talmud, as "rabbinic" and "Talmudic" Judaism. Accordingly, when we take up the problem of biography in late antiquity and deal with the quest for the holy man, critical modes of inquiry into the formative centuries of both the Christian and the Judaic components of Western civilization, we deal with an interesting question. It is how to describe, analyze, and interpret biographical materials in the context of a movement in Judaism composed of powerful personalities, yet in its literature uninterested in writing systematic and connected "lives" of those personalities. That is to say, we have out of late antiquity neither "lives" of rabbis nor personal writings by rabbis in their own names -- no biography, no autobiography or individual reflection of any kind. We do not have even writings by an individual in his own name. Why is this a paradox? It is because that movement, that system of Judaism, defined by rabbis and documented in their writings, at the same time celebrates the great man but also absorbs his statements into collective documents so framed as to obliterate distinctive traits of personality. Rabbinic circles created numerous tales about the great man, but in no way proposed to make books of those tales, narratives focused upon the individual and intended to make important points through depicting his character. The rabbis of late antiquity multiplied stories and sayings about heroes but failed to create a literary genre capable of preserving those biographical materials in a mode natural to, and comfortable with, individual character at hand.

In her splendid book, Biography in Late Antiquity. A Quest for the Holy Man (Berkeley, Los Angeles, and London, 1983: University of California Press), Patricia Cox remarks, "The biographer's task was to capture the gesture which laid bare the soul.... Ancient biographies are constellations of such gestures, carefully selected and assembled not to chronicle a life's history but to suggest its character. These character-revealing gestures are presented in the biographies primarily by means of images and anecdotes..." (p. xi). Now when we turn from Porphyry and Eusebius, with their lives of Origen and Plotinus, respectively, to the nameless authors of stories and tales about rabbis, we enter a world in which the intent is just the opposite of the one adduced by Cox. Specifically, interest in the individual character of a rabbi never defines the purpose of a story. Quite the contrary, what the story-teller wishes to convey, and what the redactor of the story proposes to accomplish by preserving the story in his composition, is how an individual exemplifies virtues held in common.

The goal of the rabbinic movement was to create holy men (women would have to wait twenty centuries for their day, which, happily, now has come). The model of holiness was always the same, namely, man in God's image, above all, the sage in the image of Moses "our rabbi." As God was one, as Moses presented a single image for all time, so the rabbi aspired to be like God, in the model Moses had brought down from on high. What place, then, for individuality? And what interest in character? Not what a hero-rabbi was, but the things he decided in the setting of Israel's sanctification, is what made a difference.

Cox states that "ancient biographies of holy men were caricatures whose aim was to evoke and thus to reveal the interior geography of the hero's life...." By contrast, in the corpus of rabbinical writings, stories about holy men proposed to illustrate and exemplify a standard applicable to all Israelites and to provoke a single effect among them.

Yet, in context, the stories at hand speak not of "a rabbi" but a named man. Clearly more than a single motive comes into play when Rabbi X is differentiated from Rabbi Y, and when tales gather around a distinct name and portray a distinctive person. To exemplify law or legal points in conflict, people did not have to tell stories about Meir and Judah. They needed only to cite their names if at issue lay only their authority. Why then tell not only what a man said, but also what he did? And why speak of individual authorities at all, when matters could be laid out in quite other forms entirely. The puzzle, then, of ancient rabbinical biography as story-tellers, framers, redactors, and transmitters of sayings and tales and comments about and in the name of particular individuals, is simple. Why speak of individuals in the setting of a religious system proposing to encourage its devotees to conform to a single pattern? And why tell such stories and yet preserve them in literary genres asymmetrical to the nature of biography to begin with?

It seems to me the way to undertake analysis of these questions is to begin with a simple question: how shall we uncover and trace the formation of the materials for biography contained within the canon of rabbinical writings of late antiquity? Specifically, we ask whether we may differentiate among the layers and levels of those biographical materials and discover traits characteristic of the one and not the other, or qualities typical of them all. In raising these questions of method, of course, I mean to explore the application of method to a given figure. In the end I aim (like Cox) at learning more about not the hero of biography but the author, or in this case, the collective authorship of the rabbinic sages themselves: how did that authorship do its work in the confrontation with an important individual. There are then these two paradoxes. The first is presented by the dissonance of biographical materials in so collective and general a corpus of writings as the rabbinical canonical documents. The second is that of anonymous authorship. Just as there is no room for a "life," but there is much material with which to compose a life, so there is no room for an individual author, but at hand (and that by definition) there is also an authorship.

I revert at the end to Cox's eloquent statement at the end of her book (pp. 148-149): "A biography is the biographer's interpretative judgment of his own dream. While he dreams, he is in that daemonic 'world between,' a threshold over which the magical and the banal, the mysterious and the mundane, cross and recross, interpreting each other and giving to their host his mythic perspective. When the biographer writes, he judges that dreaming by giving it concrete expression. He names the patterns of faces that reflect how he has conversed with the gods and with human reality, thus giving his hero's daemonic character a place to dwell. Long ago, Heraclitus said, 'a man's character is his daemon.' Character is daemonic. The biographies of Late Antiquity were living embodiments of the truth of that enigma." Cox describes a world distant from that of the sages at hand, yet the world and age in which they lived. Rabbis spoke of worldly things and in wide-awake language. Yet rabbis' writings portray speakers bearing names and so -- at least by superficial intent -- also characters and personalities. Hence, we hear something else: a voice from not the school or stoa of public discourse, but from the inner space of individual reflection. In the end, the rabbinic movement succeeded in making its own, political and public, what had, by definition, emerged from a world that was private and individual, in individuals' minds, hearts, souls. That is what the rabbinic system of Judaism aimed to accomplish: to make of Jews corporate Israel, a society that held together in its balance and proportion, a Parthenon, a Temple of sanctity and sanctification. Perhaps that is what systems always mean to do. Then women and men, individuals, always present obstacles. For, after all, they always are what they are: themselves, stubbornly, incorrigibly distinctive. I see in the rabbinic corpus, as it attends to what Rabbi X said and did, and what Rabbi Y said and did, an effort to draw into a single, whole and corporate statement what cannot be permitted to endure on its own, that moment of greatness in which, in being like God, each woman, each man is only herself, himself -- that alone.

Most of the shank of this book comes from my Eliezer ben Hyrcanus. The Tradition and the Man (Leiden, 1973: E.J. Brill) I-II. The idea of reworking some of the materials of that rather large project into a simple account for a broader readership comes to me from a number of colleagues and graduate students; it suffered the quite fair criticism of other colleagues and graduate students, and for a long time I could not see how I could reshape Eliezer into something more accessible than the original 1,000 pages. It was only after reading Professor Cox's splendid book that I perceived issues of broad and general interest in the rabbinic tales about Eliezer and sayings attributed to him. Even though much that follows turns out to be rather particular and in some place technical, I think once the larger implications of the corpus at hand strike the readers of this book, they will find important what until now has appeared to be rather special, private to a small and trivial field of learning.

Professor William S. Green, University of Rochester, was the one who saw the correspondence between the problem of the unattributed saying, dealt with in my From Mishnah to Scripture. The Problem of the Unattributed Saying (Chico, 1984), and the counterpart and mirror-image, the problem of the attributed saying. The two have to be treated together and in balance, and that is what I have tried to do in these two books. I appreciate Green's extensive discussions with me on matters of scholarship and his sharing his insight with me.

INTRODUCTION

THE PROBLEM OF THE ATTRIBUTED SAYING

All documents produced by the rabbinic movement of late antiquity -- from the first to the seventh centuries A.D. -- bear two contradictory traits of authorship. None is signed by a named individual. All bear a heavy burden of named, or attributed sayings, in which a specific authority's name is attached to a statement or made the identifying mark of a story. On the surface assigning sayings and stories to specific men (no women are involved) raises the possibility of studying the biographies -- life histories, personal characteristics, distinctive perspectives, opinions on events of the age -- of those who are named.

For more than a hundred years, from the mid-1850s to the late 1960s, scholars of Talmud history wrote such biographies. The first important ones were in Z. Frankel's Darkhe Hammishnah (1860), which presents thumbnail sketches of named persons of the Mishnah. These sketches are composed of a pastiche of tales found in diverse rabbinic compilations, early and late. The last ambitious biography in a European language in that same tradition was my Life of Yohanan ben Zakkai (1962). (Only Y.D. Gilat's work on Eliezer ben Hyrcanus has appeared since that time.) To be sure, Yeshiva-based collectors continue to publish books that assemble these same sayings and stores about given names. But their purpose is accomplished in the work of collection and arrangement and they make no pretense of scholarship in any familiar sense. It follows that attributed sayings have served to solve the problems of Talmudic biography. They have not been conceived to pose problems at all.

Now the attributions present a problem: What do they signify? How are we to use them and what do we learn, and what do we not learn, from them? Let me explain. In my Development of a Legend. Studies on the Traditions Concerning Yohanan ben Zakkai (1970), The Rabbinic Traditions about the Pharisees before 70 (1971) I-III, and Eliezer ben Hyrcanus. The Tradition and the Man (1973), and in my students' work on other authorities of the period beyond the destruction of the Temple in A.D. 70 (William Scott Green, on Joshua ben Hananiah, Gary G. Porton on Ishmael in four volumes, Joel Gereboff on Tarfon, Shammai Kanter on Gamaliel, Jack N. Lightstone on Yose the Galilean, Tzvee Zahavy on Eleazar ben Azariah, Charles Primus on Aqiba, and Robert Goldenberg on Meir, to name the principal works), a new era begins. The attributed sayings, instead of solving problems, define the issue.

Specifically, all of us ask, Do attributed sayings and stores permit us to recover the biography of the man to whom sayings are assigned and about whom stories are told? Granted that these sayings do not themselves constitute facts of biography, do they contain useful and usable facts about individuals? And, if we cannot demonstrate that they do, what other purposes may be served by studying as a distinct category of inquiry materials bearing a single name and alleged, by those responsible for hanging the name on the saying (or the saying on the name), to tell us something we would not know had said name been omitted?

Clearly, the fact that sayings are attributed makes possible a broad range of inquiries. But the place at which to begin is defined by the simplest possible datum. It is that a saying and a name have been tied together. The first question then is a narrowly biographical-historical question: What do we know that we should not otherwise have known? And what use is that knowledge? This book reports on the first systematic study of a major figure generally assigned to the period after A.D. 70, which we call the Yavnean period (after the principal center of sages' work at that time).

Two principles dictate the procedures and results of this study.

1. What we cannot show we do not know.

2. What we cannot falsify, we also cannot verify.

The first of the two is self-evident. In few fields of critical humanistic inquiry would people have to stress it. In the field at hand, ridden as it is with theological presuppositions, blighted as it has become with the pretense that true believers can also undertake serious scholarship, people maintain a different position. It is phrased in two ways.

First, from Jerusalem comes the Torah that we "have" to believe unless we can prove otherwise. That is to say, as E.E. Urbach has stated matters in various places, if we cannot demonstrate that a story is false or that a saying was not said by the person to whom it is assigned, we "have" to believe that the story is true and use it for historical purposes. We "have" to assume that the person to whom a saying is attributed really said it and use it for biographical purposes.

Second, from London comes the tocsin that there are some facts of history that we know a priori, even though we cannot demonstrate their facticity. Haim Maccoby alleges that there are things we know about the past, even though we cannot show how we know them. While he has done no work in the area at hand, he has passed his opinion ubiquitously. So he represents a viewpoint to be addressed.

Both forms of the conviction that there are things we know that we cannot show contradict the fundamental character of Western historical inquiry since the Renaissance. Urbach and Maccoby represent viewpoints that reject the lasting lessons of the Enlightenment and of nineteenth century critical historical scholarship. Only because Judaic studies in its Western form comes very late to the university scene do such viewpoints gain any hearing whatsoever, and then only when Jews treat Judaic studies as religious, national, and ethnic in focus. But we do not work in a vacuum. Since people in yeshivas, U.S. and European Jewish seminaries, and Israeli universities, who form the natural constituency for historical work on Talmudic and related literature, maintain the view that we may know what has happened in the past on some basis other than historical sources deriving from the past (revelation? what our rabbi tells us? the consensus of the learned believers?), we have to confront widely held beliefs. That is why, with this apology, I have to restate the utter banality that, in historical study, we only know what we can show.

The second proposition is a commonplace in Anglo-American philosophy, including the philosophy that reaches expression in the study of the natural world and of society, past and present, alike. It is not enough to be able to prove that what is true is true. We have also to know when what we think is true is not true. If we cannot tell the difference between what is true and what is not true, we cannot make any reliable statements. In the work at hand, I have carried out experiments which permit me to impose tests of both verification and falsification upon important aspects of a corpus of sayings that allege a given person made a given statement.

Such tests include the issues of continuity and consistency. Do sayings that appear to come early in the tradition prove cogent with one another? If not, then one group is not likely to be authentic to the person to whom they are assigned. If so, then all sayings are likely to represent a cogent viewpoint upon the philosophy of the person to whom they are assigned.

Do sayings that appear later in the formation of the tradition cohere with those assigned earlier? Do we find the attribution of sayings on topics or viewpoints with no link to what is assigned to the same person in earlier layers in the formation of the tradition? If so, then people later on appear to have been making things up. If not, then a certain discipline governed what might, and might not, be introduced later on.

Or, alternatively, if so, then a mode of transmitting sayings may have existed, in which what an earlier generation did not write down a later generation chose to take up. If not, then pretty much everything that came from the time in which the hero lived reached the next generation, and everything that came to them came into the hands of the generation beyond.

I lay out only a few among a substantial number of propositions available for validation and falsification. Clearly, this other mode of thought, in which we entertain possibilities and sort out theses for analysis and testing, will prove alien to people who concentrate on why we "have" to believe it all and then make up histories out of everything in hand. But those people have ceased to produce books in the field under study here. Coming from Israeli universities and U.S. yeshivas and seminaries is not a single book in which a major topic of Talmudic history, or a sustained biography, or a systematic account of a problem in Talmudic law viewed historically or Talmudic theology read in the context of late antiquity, is taken up. In a decade and a half there has been nothing sustained, nothing encompassing, nothing of weight. Approaches other than the humanistic and critical ones have fallen silent. It is hardly an exaggeration to declare bankrupt all approaches founded on conviction of an-other-than academic character. Proof, as I said, is that people have simply stopped working on major projects, sustained and systematic books. The exceptions are so few as to change nothing. That is why there is so little debate on the issues at hand, but so much abuse.

Let me now point to an important statement on correct method in historical epistemology -- what we know and how we know in historical study -- deriving from a different field from the one at hand. What follows is a brilliant and concise statement of everything right in contemporary historical method by K.R. Walters, the distinguished classicist at Wayne State University. In an article remote from the interests of the present work, Walters comments on a mode of thought characteristic of work in ancient history. This is what he says (in "Perikles' Citizenship Law," Classical Antiquity 1983, 2:315-316):

> Standard procedure in historical research is to form a hypothesis on the basis of a few facts, often intuitively, and then to search for additional data to support the hypothesis, now that one knows what to look for. This involves a logical fallacy and a kind of circularity of reasoning. Namely, the first inference is: if my hypothesis is correct, then such and such data exist (formally, if H, then D_1, D_2, D_3,... D_n). When the data are found, this is reversed into: if such and such data exist, then my hypothesis is correct (e.g., if D_1, D_2, D_3,... D_n, then H). Not only is this procedure, technically speaking, the fallacy of affirming the consequent, it is, even if repaired into the modus ponens (if D, then H; D, therefore H) inadequate for strengthening a hypothesis in an inductive science such as history. [Walter notes: In fact, the modus ponens is never really used in historical research, that is, historians never proceed purely from data to hypothesis, but always form a hypothesis first, decide what kind of data would support it, and then go searching for that evidence. In strict logical terms, the discovery of that evidence does not "prove" the hypothesis. For this position and an examination of the issues involved, C. Popper, Conjectures and Refutations (New York 1968) 33-59, is still pertinent.] That is because, no matter how much data one gathers in support of a given hypothesis, there is always the possibility of neglected data turning up that will refute the hypothesis or of data taken to be supportive turning out to imply a consequence that contradicts (and thus invalidates) the hypothesis, just the method that Sokrates so often used to confute his adversaries. What in fact strengthens a hypothesis to to seek by all possible means to disconfirm it (the modus tollens: if H, then D; not D, therefore not H). The more one is unable to come up with contrary data to refute the hypothesis, the greater the likelihood that the hypothesis is true. As will become clear from this paper, it is the failure to anticipate and deflect potentially negative data or the negative implications of data already used to support a given theory that undermines many of the theories so far put forth about the meaning and motivation of Perikles' citizenship law. In the final analysis a rigorous skepticism is the ancient historian's most powerful methodological tool.

What Walters says lays out the program of the present work. What I want to know is how to trace the unfolding of the history of sayings and stories in the name of an important first century rabbi. To work out that history I have to discover tests not of validation or verification alone but also of falsification: how do I know when I am right? how do I know when I am wrong? how do I tell the difference? I believe that in Eliezer ben Hyrcanus: The Tradition and the Man I made considerable progress in developing tests of validation and falsification. In fact, once that work was completed, I reached the conclusion that, for the moment, I could progress no further. That is why I turned to a quite separate set of problems, which occupied me from 1972, when Eliezer was done, through 1981, when I had completed my history of the law of the Mishnah and the associated synthetic studies culminating in Judaism: The Evidence of the Mishnah (Chicago, 1981: University of Chicago Press).

Let me now place into context the study of sayings attributed to Eliezer ben Hyrcanus and stories told about him accomplished in the original work and given in precis in the present book.

The work on Eliezer continues the inquiry into the history of the rabbinic tradition in late antiquity begun with Development of a Legend: Studies on the Traditions Concerning Yohanan ben Zakkai (Leiden, 1970: E.J. Brill), and continued in The Rabbinic Traditions about the Pharisees before 70. I. The Masters. II. The Houses. III. Conclusions (Leiden, 1971: E.J. Brill). Its problem is to trace the development of a sample body of rabbinic tradition, to analyze the literary traits of the various sayings and stories, to see whether we can locate characteristic techniques, forms, and tendencies in the formation of various sorts of materials -- in all, to develop a critical structure and system. At the end are offered some firm conclusions on the historical Eliezer b. Hyrcanus.

Before that sequence of books students of rabbinic literature routinely assigned pretty much equal historical value to all sources, without regard to the date of the compilation or collection in which they appear. Exceptions to the rule are episodic, never systematic. Thus a story first occurring in a compilation of midrashim attested at the earliest in the fourteenth century and one first found in Tosefta were generally given equal weight. Further, it was always taken for granted that we deal with an essentially consistent, unitary tradition. Therefore all stories must be brought (or forced) into agreement with one another. Differences of viewpoint or of emphasis, where they are even recognized (and this was primarily in the legal, not in the biographic or theological-exegetical materials) were bypassed or ignored or harmonized. At no point was the question raised, Is it possible that several groups, even in the time of the single master under discussion, had several different opinions about him, not to mention traditions in his name? Just as the texts -- e.g., Mishnah, Tosefta -- were seen as essentially unitary documents, so the stories and sayings told about, or attributed to, a given authority were taken for granted to be essentially unitary accounts, consistent traditions, from undifferentiated sources or authorities.

In Development of a Legend, for the first time ever, I undertook to show by comparison of the forms and versions of all the stories told about one master, that materials found in a document close to his life and times are apt to be historically more reliable than what first occurs in a document attested only long afterward. The traditions about Yohanan ben Zakkai are not substantial, however, and while the comparison of the several versions of each story or saying often revealed what seemed to be later emendations, omissions, or additions, the total result was limited.

In The Rabbinic Traditions about the Pharisees before 70 I carried the study much further, first, by pointing out that a saying may be shown to have been known to an authority before its occurrence in a later document. Consideration of such attestations, proposed in Phar. III, pp. 180-238, resulted in the division of the rabbinic traditions about the Pharisees into the legal sayings attributed to the Houses, the themes of which often are first attested in Yavneh, and stores about specific, named masters as well as legal materials attributed to them, first known in later times, beginning with the Ushan stratum. It further appeared that the historiographical traditions about the pre-70 Pharisees came to the fore in Ushan times and proved astonishingly pertinent to the theological and political situation of Usha itself.

A second important result was the effort to propose a theory of the history of fixed forms for the formulation and transmission of traditions.

In the present work I refine the methods developed in the former studies, both by reconsidering earlier results, and by developing, through the application to new, and more complex materials, the approaches employed in the earlier studies. The traditions about Eliezer b. Hyrcanus prove extremely complicated and demand the revision and refinement of all former procedures. They represent the first really substantial body of attested materials on an individual master. In quantity they far exceed the whole of the rabbinic traditions about pre-70 masters and are nearly equal to those traditions as well as the ones about the Houses of Shammai and Hillel. In quality they bring us to a quite new situation, in which we have some idea of how traditions were handed on, when and where they were shaped, and what influences affected their formation.

Eliezer b. Hyrcanus stands, along with Joshua b. Hananiah, as the first major figure after 70 in the preserved materials. From the other early Yavneans, for instance, Saddoq and his son Eleazar, Tarfon, as well as those who, beside Eliezer and Joshua, are said to have been disciples of Yohanan b. Zakkai -- Yosi the Priest, Eleazar b. 'Arakh, and Simeon b. Nathaniel -- no important, independent traditions have come down to us. If Gamaliel was a youngster at the outset of the Yavnean period, then he cannot represent the situation in the very beginning. Eliezer's traditions exceed in quantity and in originality those assigned to Joshua; and Joshua's materials stand close, in many respects, to Aqiba's. So with Eliezer we begin the study of a very large and rich corpus of sayings and stories concerning a figure early in the formation of the rabbinic system of Judaism.

Let me now explain the present work, a precis and abbreviation of the original one. We begin, in Chapter One, with an extended sample of legal materials in which Eliezer b. Hyrcanus is cited. I have given a number of examples out of the much larger corpus -- 500 printed pages -- of Eliezer ben Hyrcanus. The Tradition and the Man. I. The Tradition. I think it important for the reader to confront the texts (in translation) so as to assess exactly how the documents at hand propose to tell us about an individual, his opinions and his deeds. In my comments on the several cited passages, I systematically raise a set of critical questions on the viewpoint of the pericope at hand. In the original work I present translations of the entire corpus; the selections here seem to me representative and important.

Proceeding to Eliezer ben Hyrcanus. II. The Man, we turn, in Chapters Two through Four, to lay the groundwork for the exercises of reconstruction in Chapters Five through Seven. In the former I distinguish among the sayings attributed to, and stories about, Eliezer ben Hyrcanus. This I do in accord with simple criteria. If sayings bear comments, external to the structure in which those sayings stand, in the names of sages who lived before A.D. 135, that is to say, within a generation of Eliezer himself, I categorize those sayings as "best." They are best by comparison to another set, those in the category of "better" traditions. These are marked by comments by authorities who lived after A.D. 135. Those commentators cannot have known Eliezer personally or have received from Eliezer's immediate circle of disciples information on his views and activities. In the same chapter I treat, in addition, "fair" traditions, that is to say, statements assigned to Eliezer or stores told about him that appear, without prior comment or attestation, in the documents of the end of the second century, principally the Mishnah. (I treat Tosefta as integral to the Mishnah, hence "Mishnah-Tosefta.") These "fair" traditions then can be shown to have circulated only in the document in which they first appear and not before that time, by contrast to the "best" and the "better" traditions.

In the next two chapters I survey all of the traditions that fall into the categories outlined in the foregoing. To each set of traditions I address a single set of questions, indicated in the table of contents. In the final chapter I treat the materials about Eliezer ben Hyrcanus that make their first appearance only in later documents, the two Talmuds and the compilations of scriptural exegeses in particular. I briefly address to these same essentially unattested and legendary materials, appearing centuries after Eliezer's life, the same questions introduced earlier. The upshot is a complete account of the way in which the rabbinic documents appear in sequence to portray a single first century rabbi.

Since this book provides a precis and abbreviation of a much larger (and more complex) work, I make reference in what follows to sources that the reader will not have in hand. The examples given in Chapter One cover only a few of the hundreds of individual entries concerning Eliezer ben Hyrcanus in the composite of the rabbinic canon, beginning to end. In my Eliezer ben Hyrcanus (II, pp. 1-17) I catalogue well over three hundred distinct entries, many of them occurring in variant forms in successive documents. I have to beg the reader's indulgence in allowing me to allude to materials not found in the pages of this book. It is the only way I could proceed. I do summarize the substance of many passages. In the reconstructions of Chapters Five, Six, and Seven, I make ample reference to most of the items laid out in the original work. But readers who want to consult the sources and to learn more about them will have to refer to the larger work epitomised here.

CHAPTER ONE
A SELECTION OF SOURCES ABOUT ELIEZER BEN HYRCANUS

i. Legal Traditions

A. From what time do they read the Shema in the evening?

B. From the hour that the priests enter to eat their Heave-offering.

C. "Until the end of the first watch" -- the words of R. Eliezer.
And sages say, "Until midnight."
Rabban Gamaliel says, "Until the morning star rises."

D. M'SH S: his [Gamaliel's] sons came from the banquet house. They said to him, "We have not read the Shema."
He said to them, "If the morning star has not risen, you are obligated (HYYBYN) [Kaufmann, Parma: Permitted] to read [it]."

E. And not this only, but in all matters concerning which the sages have said, "Until midnight" -- their obligation [persists] until the morning star rises.
Burning the fat and the limbs -- their obligation [persists] until the morning star rises. And all which is to be eaten in one day -- their obligation [persists] until the morning star rises.
If so, why have the sages said, "Until midnight?" In order to keep a man far from sin.

M. Ber. 1:1

A. From what time do they read the Shema in the morning?
From the time that one may distinguish between blue and white.

B. R. Eliezer says, "Between blue and green."

C. [Camb., Parma omit:] And he completes it before sunrise.

D. R. Joshua says, "Before the third hour."

E. "For it is the way of princes to arise at the third hour."

F. He who reads thenceforward has not lost, like a man who is reading in the Torah.

M. Ber. 1:2

Comment: The dispute of Eliezer, the sages, and Gamaliel pertains only to the second clause, until. No party refers to the first part of the answer to the question. From the hour -- Heave-offering serves equally well -- or poorly -- to introduce the opinions of all three parties, for parts A and B are complete in themselves. The question is not, until when, but from when -- and that question is answered by B. Part C introduces a new issue. But it begins without a superscription, <u>Until when do they read the Shema in the evening</u>?

The same structure is evident in M. Ber. 1:1. Part A asks, <u>From what time</u>, and <u>that</u> question is answered. Eliezer then glosses. Part C completes the pericope: <u>they read from the time... until before sunrise</u>. Then Joshua glosses. Part E extends Joshua's saying by explaining his reasoning, but it clearly is an interpolation, for Joshua's saying is as brief as Eliezer's here, and in M. Ber. 1:1 the three opinions are carefully matched: <u>Until 1. end 2. midnight 3. morning star</u>. Thus in both instances the form is as follows:

1.	Question	<u>From when</u> --
2.	[Anonymous] answer	<u>Until</u> -- [and he completes it...]
3.	Yavnean gloss	

M. Ber. 1:1: Eliezer, sages, Gamaliel

M. Ber. 1:2: Eliezer to part A, Joshua to part C.

The present form therefore leads to the supposition that before the Yavnean masters was a segment of a completed code of law, entirely anonymous, of which this segment was subject to discussion. That code would have consisted of the following:

<u>From when do they read</u>... evening
From the hour that the priests...
[And he completes it before...]
<u>From when do they read</u>... morning
From [the time] that he may distinguish...
<u>And he completes it before</u>...

The first <u>And he completes it before</u> has been lost. We cannot now guess what the Temple rule would have been. It has been set aside by C. The form left no room for a simple gloss, as in M. Ber. 1:2, <u>And he completes it before... R. Joshua says, Before</u>..., because a whole set of opinions, not a single gloss, was in hand. So I would guess that the original version had an appropriate conclusions, on the time beyond which one no longer says the <u>Shema</u>. The further, anonymous rules in M. Ber. 1:4 and 1:5 would evidently form part of the Temple rule. The Houses' pericope (M. Ber. 1:3, see <u>Phar.</u> II, p. 41) would then represent the first Pharisaic-rabbinic stage of commentary, the early Yavneans' glosses, the second.

Evidently the antecedent code derives from the Temple, for it demarcates time by the priestly service -- eating Heave-offering. Then the Yavneans change the imagery, choosing not Temple rites but routine, secular times -- first watch, midnight, morning star -- which anyone, not merely priests, would understand. But the Temple-imagery recurs in the extended gloss, e.g., burning the fat and the limbs, and is preserved in later strata.

Part D then ignores Eliezer's opinion. It is from a Gamalielite hand, for it harmonizes the sages' opinion with his: the sages really agree with him that it is legitimate to do the various commandments until dawn, but have ruled strictly in order to prevent people from sinning. Therefore Gamaliel and the sages really are in agreement. The counsel Gamaliel gave to his sons was correct -- but not under normal circumstances. This leaves Eliezer out; no one bothers to harmonize his opinion, which could have supported the same rationalization. So part D is introduced by a Gamalielite, and part D then harmonizes the sages of C with the story of D. E comes last of all. Before the intrusion of D, it is pointless to say, "and not this only," explicitly referring to the story in D. Standing by itself, moreover, it still depends upon Gamaliel's opinion, therefore probably also upon the story.

The present story obviously would have stood outside of the narrow framework of commentary on the priestly law. The first stage, therefore, would be C, then D and E follow, all within the circle of Gamaliel. On the other hand, we have noticed that named masters before 70, except Hananiah Prefect of the Priests and Gamaliel I, normally do not have legal sayings in standard legal form. Their legal opinions come in the form of stories or attributions, which then may be generalized into Rabbi X says... form. So it is not out of the question that Gamaliel's original opinion was preserved as the story, D, which yielded the saying in C, followed by equally terse formulations for opinions of Eliezer and the sages, whose stories -- if any existed -- were simply dropped.

All glosses of the original code are extremely terse -- simply completions of the original sentence, therefore depending upon it for context and meaning. Eliezer in M. Ber. 1:2B and Joshua in M. Ber. 1:2D simply take up the language of M. Ber. 1:2A and C, respectively, and revise its operative clause.

We must ask, finally, whether mnemonic considerations have governed the formulation of pericopae. As for M. Ber. 1:1 A and B and M. Ber. 1:2 A and C, I see no effort at placing the whole into a single, simple pattern for easy memorization, other than the use of questions and answers. But M. Ber. 1:1 C introduces all opinions with the same word, 'D, and then arranges them in thematically appropriate order: the earliest, middle, and latest time to be specified. The story follows in simple narrative style -- which is not a discipline form -- but which, as usual, relies on a topic sentence to set the stage, then on dialogue to unfold the story. The long gloss in M. Ber. 1:1 E and the shorter one in M. Ber. 1:2 E seem to be simple declarative sentences, without mnemonic formulae.

A.   They mention "the Power of rain" in "Resurrection of the dead," and ask
     for rain in the "Blessing of the Years."

B.   And Havdalah --
     In "Favors [man with] knowledge."

C.   R. Aqiba says, "He says it as a fourth blessing, by itself."

D.   R. Eliezer says, "In 'Thanksgiving.'"

M. Ber. 5:2

Comment: Aqiba and Eliezer differ from the anonymous rule in B. No one alludes to A, on which all parties agree. The anonymous opinion (B) is that on Saturday night one says <u>Havdalah</u> in the fourth blessing, that beginning with the words "You favor man with knowledge." Aqiba maintains that the <u>Havdalah</u> is said by itself and has its own concluding blessing, "Blessed... who distinguishes sacred and profane." Then the blessing normally standing at fourth place, "Favors man with knowledge," is said, now as the fifth. Eliezer says the <u>Havdalah</u> is recited in the "Thanksgiving" prayer, after the normal Eighteen Blessings have been concluded. So Aqiba is in disagreement with the anonymous opinion, and Eliezer stands outside the range of that disagreement.

Aqiba's saying depends upon B but expands the saying: he <u>says it</u>. The simplest structure would be, <u>And [as to] Havdalah, he says it in "Favors"... As "Blessing"... In "Thanksgiving."</u> This was impossible because the opening sentence is a complete thought: <u>They make mention... They ask... And [they say] Havdalah... They say</u> thus is understood. But to introduce Aqiba's saying, the redactor has had to supply what formerly was understood, so as to separate the dispute from the materials on which all parties stand in agreement. Then Eliezer's saying remains in its brief, "original" form, a single-word-reference to the appropriate place in the service, <u>In (B)+Blessing</u>.

The two named masters therefore differ with reference to a detail of an already completed pericope, to which their sayings in C + D add a gloss. One must again wonder, therefore, what stood before them, and from what source they derived the rules on which they agreed -- in the <u>very</u> language now before us?

Perhaps an antecedent code was worked out and handed on to Yavneh; or perhaps Yavneans gave as anonymous law the decisions on which all parties agreed. Here the difference between the two possibilities is a real one. The issue of the anonymous law, A, suggests that someone was working out fundamental issues of liturgy. Perhaps some basic structure of prayer was received at Yavneh, and the Yavnean masters then had to work out and insert some details of the new prayers they proposed to supply -- a prayer for rain, <u>Havdalah</u>, and so forth. Alternatively, the Yavneans were working out a quite new liturgy, and the antecedent materials on which Eliezer and Aqiba comment were the work of their generation alone. I see no grounds for coming to a firm conjecture.

The antecedent rule -- One does not stand up to pray except with proper reverence -- contains a tradition about the early pious men (<u>Hasidim HaRishonim</u>). But that tradition interpolates information not essential to the opening rule, and then M. Ber. 5:2 begins with language in the same form as M. Ber. 5:1, "They do not stand... They make mention... They ask..." M. Ber. 5:3 has a quite separate rule, unrelated in substance, and in different sentence-structure, "He who says... They silence him. He who passes before the ark and errs..." So the opening paragraphs preserve consistent usage, which changes afterward.

This would seem to indicate that M. Ber. 5:1-2 are to be distinguished from M. Ber. 5 :3ff., and are a separate unit; without the reference to the early pious men, the form would be consistent with M. Ber. 1:1,2: the present participle, in the plural, <u>From what time do they</u>...

Let us assemble all rules that make use of this simple construction:

M. Ber. 1:1: From what time do they read the Shema in the evening.

M. Ber. 1:2: From what time do they read the Shema in the morning.

[M. Ber. 1:3: House of Shammai vs. House of Hillel on proper posture for Shema, interpolated into foregoing.]

M. Ber. 1:5: They mention the Exodus from Egypt at night. [Drop: Interpolation of Eleazar b. Azariah.]

M. Ber. 2:3: Women, slaves, and children are free of the obligation to read Shema.

M. Ber. 1:5: They rise to say the Prayer only with reverence.

M. Ber. 5:2: They make mention...

So the pericopae which make use of the present tense participle in the plural pertain to reading the Shema and saying the Prayer. It would then seem that the original "code" alluded to above contained simple rules about saying the Shema and the Prayer in the morning. It has been abbreviated -- surely other rules existed -- but at the same time richly interpolated by rabbinic rules of various kinds. But none of these is given in the simple plural, present-participial form; whether or not assigned to named masters, all make use of forms different from the basic one.

Now let us now look for the same simple construction in the subsequent chapters:

M. Ber. 6:1: How do they bless fruit?

    1. Fruit from tree

    2. Wine.

    3. Fruit from earth.

    4. Bread.

    5. And vegetables (reverts to 3)

M. Ber. 6:6: [They were sitting to eat] -- Each one blesses for himself.

M. Ber. 7:3: How do they invite [for Grace]?

Various cases.

M. Ber. 8:6: They do not bless over the light, spice, of gentiles, etc.

In general, where the pericopae diverge from this simple participial structure, they also introduce special cases, exceptions, rules assigned to named masters, and the like. So the present-tense-plural-participial-pericopae supply the following rules: 1. Reciting the Shema; 2. Saying the Prayer; 3. Blessing fruit; 4. Saying Grace after meals -- the fundamentals of the ordinary Jew's liturgical life. All other materials differ both as to form and as to substance; in the former, all sorts of other constructions except this one are used, as to the latter, many kinds of special cases and other sorts of information are supplied.

Are we then able to claim a particular authority for the legal style we have here isolated? I think not. This construction is commonplace. When we consider its chief grammatical characteristic -- the use of the present participle in the plural -- we find the same construction with reference to the Houses, and in every subsequent stratum. Hence the participial construction, by itself, is merely a technique in the presentation of law (to be sure, a technique absent in Scripture). But use of that technique cannot have been limited to a single stratum or circle of masters or redactors. What recognition of the technique does permit, however, is the isolation of a stratum within a complex set of pericopae, such as a tractate of Mishnah, and here the picture is clear, as given. Since the earliest Yavneans -- Eliezer, Joshua, Gamaliel, and Aqiba -- attest to the existence, in the exact form before us, of pericopae following the plural-present-tense-participial construction, we may reliably claim that the form of simple rules given in that construction comes before their catechism, or rule book, produced by Temple authorities, but perhaps widely used outside of the Temple, has been taken over by Yavneans and employed as the basic structure for the development of their legal materials, finally redacted as Mishnah tractate Berakhot.

A.   ["An important general rule have they said concerning the Seventh Year: Whatever is gathered solely as food for man may not be used as an emollient [MLGM') for man... or cattle; and whatever is not solely for food for man may be used as an emollient for man, but not for cattle; and whatever is not solely either for food for man or for food for cattle -- if he intended it for food for man and for food for cattle, they place on it the stringent rules regarding man and cattle..." -- [M. Shev. 8:1.]

B.   A hide which one has anointed with oil of the Seventh Year --

C.   R. Eliezer says, "It is to be burned."

D.   And sages say, "He should eat [produce of] equal value (Y'KL KNGDW)."

E.   They said before R. Aqiba, "R. Eliezer used to say, 'A hide which one has anointed with oil of the Seventh Year -- it is to be burned.'

F.   He said to them, "Silence. I shall not say to you what R. Eliezer says concerning it."

M. Shev. 8:9

A.   Further they said before him, "R. Eliezer used to say, "He who eats the bread of Samaritans is like him who eats the flesh of a pig."

B.   He said to them, "Silence. I shall not tell you what R. Eliezer says concerning it."

M. Shev. 8:10

Comment: The general rule is as given in A. R. Eliezer then rules strictly; the punishment is the burning of the whole hide. M. Shev. 8:8 has, "Vessels may not be anointed with oil from Seventh Year produce, and if one has done so he must buy and consume produce of equal value." So Eliezer's ruling in C stands in opposition to the earlier, anonymous law, whose ruling then is repeated verbatim in D.

Parts E and F constitute a separate tradition. M. Shev. 8:9 and 8:10A are similar in structure; F and B are identical. So a single form has been used for two separate laws, concerning which it is stated that Eliezer's real ruling differs from the publicly acknowledged one.

Since M. Shev. 8:9E+F are virtually identical in substance to B+C, one must ask, Which comes first, the story or the generalized rule of law? Clearly, from Aqiba's words we may suppose Eliezer is dead; therefore the redactor comes later than Eliezer himself. Further, M. Shev. 8:10 has no general rule attributed to Eliezer, only a story which ought to have yielded a standard legal saying. So it does not seem as though Eliezer's opinion in M. Shev. 8:10 has produced the appropriate legal structure, and this would suggest that the story-form for his opinion comes before the standard legal saying-form. If so, M. Shev. 8:9E+F come before and produce not only B-C-D, but also M. Shev. 8:8, a still more generalized version of the sages' view (D).

M. A.Z. 2:6 contains an appropriate saying, without attribution to Eliezer and without allusion to the Samaritans (!): "These things of the gentiles are forbidden, but it is not forbidden to have any benefit at all from them [one may sell, but not consume them]: ...their bread and their oil." This anonymous rule takes for granted that idolators' bread may not be eaten. Eliezer's saying is phrased in such strong language that it invites a contrary view, "And sages say, Permitted." But the issue is not whether idolators' bread is acceptable, but Samaritans', and here the problem is the status of Samaritans, not merely of their bread. We observe in M. Dem. 5:9 an equivalent viewpoint on Eliezer's part, though it is uncertain whether in fact that is our Eliezer.

Now one must ask, What has happened to Eliezer's "real" opinion? Aqiba claims it is not as represented in M. Shev. 8:9C and 10A. Then how did the students know what they claimed to have as a tradition from Eliezer? Presumably someone has taught them an opinion in Eliezer's name, but it cannot be Aqiba. Then it is either Eliezer himself, or some other of his disciples -- Joshua is out of the question. Now Aqiba has a teaching different from that of another of Eliezer's (nameless) disciples.

What was Aqiba's teaching? It was either more strict or more lenient that the one now attributed to Eliezer. In M. Shev. 8:9 a more strict opinion is simply out of the question -- one cannot do more than destroy the hide.

If it then was a more lenient opinion, two possibilities present themselves; first is the opinion now given anonymously in M. Shev. 8:8, and to "sages" in 8:9: one buys and consumes produce of equal value. Second, he may have a still _more_ lenient opinion than the sages. Such an opinion would be that one is not punished for using Seventh Year oil for anointing hides; that is what the oil is intended for to begin with. So to Eliezer might have been attributed a statement that what is normally used for anointing may be used for anointing in the Seventh Year, as in M. Shev. 8:2: "Seventh Year produce is intended for use as food, drink, or unguent; that is to be used as food which is customarily eaten, and

that used as drink which is customarily drunk; and that used as unguent which is customarily used for anointing."

Now this is not wholly consistent with 8:1: What is customarily gathered for food
may not be used for ointment, etc. It is the generalization at the end which is set aside,
"Whatsoever is not usually gathered solely as food for man or as food for cattle, yet was
intended as food both for man and for cattle, the more stringent rules affecting both man
and cattle apply." This leaves room for cattle but does not tell us what those rules of
cattle are. So M. Shev. 8:2 -- silent on that point -- tells us, "That which is used as
unguent which is customarily used for anointing" continues to be sued for that purpose in
the Seventh Year. 8:8 applies to vessels, as we saw. Nothing is said about cattle, let
alone hides. Eliezer's rule may have been As to cattle and hides, what is customarily used
for anointing may be used for anointing in the Seventh Year.

Of these two possibilities, which seems more likely? Aqiba threatens to tell the
disciples what Eliezer had really said -- and ends by saying nothing. So something
radically different is to be attributed to him, and this, it would seem, may be the most
lenient ruling of all. Likewise with the Samaritans -- Eliezer is said to have forbidden
eating their bread; in M. Dem. 5:9/Tos. Dem. 5:22, Eliezer/Eleazar is represented as
regarding Samaritan tithing practice as similar to Israelite practice. So why not eat their
bread? If Aqiba dismisses the disciples' traditions, and those traditions are a stringent as
possible, then the alternative traditions ought to have been lenient, perhaps more lenient
than other opinions, therefore Eliezer permits eating Samaritan bread or some such view,
opposite to what the disciples say, ought to be Eliezer's real opinion.

A.   They do not give Heave-offering from what is clean for what is unclean,
      and if they gave Heave-offering, their Heave-offering is Heave-of-
      fering. [There intervenes a long interpolation, in which the consequences
      of this ruling are spelled out in terms of various details.]

B.   R. Eliezer says, "They do give Heave-offering from what is clean for
      what is unclean."

C.   [They do not give Heave-offering from unclean for clean (produce).]

                                   M. Ter. 2:1

Comment: Warrant for assigning M. Ter. 2:1 to Eliezer b. Hyrcanus is in Tos. Ter.
3:18. Eliezer differs with the anonymous opinion of A. The difference is not substantial,
for both agree that, once given, the Heave-offering is valid. The issue is whether, to
begin with, one does so. The anonymous ruling (C) proceeds:

      They do not give Heave-offering from the unclean for what is clean.
And if he gave Heave-offering --
      Accidentally -- His Heave-offering is Heave-offering.
      Intentionally -- He has done nothing.

                                   M. Ter. 2:2A

This repeats, and spells out, the position of M. Ter. 2:1A. Eliezer is not mentioned; perhaps he would see a distinction between 2:1 and 2:2, for he agrees one does not give from worse for better produce.

Does Eliezer here gloss a pre-existing rule? Or is his opinion formulated at the same point as the contrary view? It is a strikingly fundamental question. Since the Pharisees for several generations had observed the tithing rules and those of ritual uncleanness, one must wonder how it was that for so long no one had known whether one may give Heave-offering for unclean out of clean produce. M. Hal. 2:8 has the following:

> R. Eliezer says, "It [Hallah] is taken from the clean for the unclean."
> [There follows a long interpolation, explaining how one does so.]
> And sages prohibit.

In the form of M. Hal. 2:8, Eliezer differs from his contemporaries. In M. Ter. 2:1, he differs from a (pre-existing) anonymous rule. But the difference is about the same principle.

If, as in M. Ber., we isolate rules phrased in plural-present-tense-participles we find the following:

> M. Ter. 1:4: They do not give Heave-offering from olives for oil, or grapes for wine; and if they gave Heave-offering, the House of Shammai say, "It may still be deemed Heave-offering for the olives or grapes" (so Danby).
> The House of Hillel say, "Their Heave-offering is not Heave-offering."
> M. Ter. 1:5: They do not give Heave-offering from Gleanings, Forgotten Sheaf, Corner of the field, ownerless produce, etc.
> M. Ter. 1:7: They do not give Heave-offering by measure, weight, number, etc.
> M. Ter. 1:8: They do not give Heave-offering of oil for crushed olives, and if they have done so, the Heave-offering is Heave-offering, but Heave-offering must again be given. (And of these two Heave-offerings, the first renders other produce into which it may fall subject to the law of Heave-offering, etc., but this is not so with the second) [so Danby].

This seems to me decisive evidence that Eliezer differs from a pre-existing law -- a law known to the Houses, but which ought to come before them as well.

Eliezer then is the only authority who differs from the fundamental principle spelled out in the list above, carefully restricting Heave-offering to the exact produce for which the Heave-offering is given, and not mixing various forms of the same produce, e.g., olives with oil, for the purpose of giving the Heave-offering. Eliezer alone favors breaking down the rigid principle of separation in giving Heave-offering. One cannot conclude other than that he was breaking new ground. It would further seem not excessive to view Eliezer as the firm <u>terminus ante quem</u> for the entire set of 'YN TWRMYN-rules.

M. Hal. 2:8's dispute is 'artificial.' Eliezer's rule has required the inclusion of "the sages," who, in this instance, represent virtually the whole antecedent tradition!

A. R. Eliezer says, "Heave-offering is neutralized [So Danby for 'WLH] in a hundred and one [parts]."

B. R. Joshua says, "In one hundred and [a bit] more."

C. And this <u>more</u> has no [exact] measure...

M. Ter. 4:7

A. R. Joshua says, "Black figs neutralize white, and white neutralize black. Large cakes of figs neutralize small, and small neutralize large. Round cakes neutralize square, and square neutralize round."

B. R. Eliezer prohibits.

C. R. Aqiba says, "If what fell into [the mixture] is known, they do not neutralize one another. If what fell in is not known, they <u>do</u> neutralize one another."

M. Ter. 4:8

A. How so? Fifty white figs and fifty black figs --
    The black fell in --
    The black are prohibited and the white permitted.

B. [If] the white fell in --
    The white are prohibited and the black are permitted.

C. If what fell in is not known --
    They neutralize one another.

D. And in this instance, R. Eliezer is stringent, and R. Joshua lenient.

M. Ter. 4:9

A. And in this R. Eliezer is lenient and R. Joshua strict:

B. In [a case in which] he stuffed a <u>litra</u> of dried [Heave-offering] figs into the mouth of a jar, and he does not know which one --

C. R. Eliezer says, "We regard them as if they were separated figs, and the ones on the bottom neutralize those on the top."

M. Ter. 4:10

A. A <u>se'ah</u> of Heave-offering which fell into the mouth of a store-jar, and he skimmed it off--

B. R. Eliezer says, "If in the layer removed were a hundred <u>se'ahs</u>, it is neutralized in one hundred and one."

C. And R. Joshua says, "It is not neutralized."

D.   A se'ah of Heave-offering which fell into the mouth of a store-jar, he
     should skim it off.

E.   If so, why have they said that Heave-offering is neutralized in one
     hundred and one [parts]?
     [That applies only] if it is not known whether they are mixed up, or
     where it fell [= M. Ter. 4:8C].

                          M. Ter. 4:11

Comment: While earlier, Eliezer would permit clean Heave-offering to be given for
unclean, here he does not allow different colored figs to neutralize one another, so that
Heave-offering may be given for the whole. That principle would seem to be inconsistent
with the earlier ruling.

M. Ter. 4:7: If a qav of Heave-offering falls into a hundred of unconsecrated
produce, the Heave-offering is neutralized; new Heave-offering is given, but the mixture
is permitted. Joshua differs on a minute quantity -- something less than a qav is
sufficient. The opinions are unbalanced:

Eliezer: 'HD WM'H

Joshua: M'H W'WD

So the difference is 'HD vs. 'WD -- not a very striking syzygy.

M. Ter. 4:8: If a fig of Heave-offering -- whether white or black -- fell into a
hundred of unconsecrated produce, of which fifty are white and fifty are black, those two
fifties join together to neutralize the fig of Heave-offering, even though if it was a black
fig, the white ones are not conceivably forbidden, for among them is no white Heave-of-
fering-fig. Joshua permits that the fig be neutralized in this situation. In his opinion
Heave-offering is neutralized by a mere majority of unconsecrated food. The sages
required a hundred and one. If the whole mixture has that larger quantity, it suffices.
And so in the other (unnecessary) examples.

Eliezer prohibits, for the figs which are not in doubt do not join together to
neutralize the Heave-offering.

Aqiba's position is explained in M. Ter. 4:9. If we know for certain that the
Heave-offering fig was white (or black), then it will not be neutralized in the mixture of
fifty white and fifty black figs. But if not, they do. His position seems to be a compromise -- but in fact favors Eliezer. That is, where we know for sure (as in Joshua's
case, M. Ter. 4:8), then the mixture will not neutralize the Heave-offering. Where we do
not know for sure which is which, then all are in doubt -- and so Aqiba stands with Eliezer.

M. Ter. 4:9D therefore accurately refers the dispute of A-C back to Eliezer, for it is
Eliezer's position which Aqiba has espoused.

M. Ter. 4:10 speaks of a jar in which there are one hundred litras of unconsecrated
dry figs. The man does not know into which jar he has stuffed the Heave-offering.

Eliezer says one regards the figs in all the jars as if they are not stuck together, but
loose. They therefore are all regarded as mixed together and serve to neutralize the litra
of dried figs of Heave-offering which are on the top of the jar, even though the figs on the

bottom in no sense are in doubt as to the prohibition of Heave-offering. Under any circumstances the fig of Heave-offering is on the mouth of the jar. But as to black/white, we <u>know</u> the Heave-offering fig is one or the other -- so Albeq, <u>Seder Zera'im</u>, p. 191.

Joshua says that only if we have a hundred jars is this Heave-offering neutralized by the hundred others. But the ones on the bottom do not mix together with the one(s) on the top and therefore do not neutralize the other -- unlike the white/black, where they are mixed together.

The language of the two masters is not matched. Each responds directly to the topic sentence, but only inferentially to the other.

<u>M. Ter. 4:11</u> now introduces the case of wheat, a <u>se'ah</u> of Heave-offering of which has fallen into the mouth of a store-jar. Then the top layer was skimmed off.

Eliezer rules that if in the removed layer were a hundred <u>se'ahs</u>, the <u>se'ah</u> of Heave-offering is neutralized in a hundred and one. Joshua says it has not been neutralized. Eliezer thus does not claim that the lower rows of grain are joined to make one hundred <u>se'ahs</u>.

Joshua says that since the man is obligated to remove the <u>se'ah</u>, it is impossible to claim it will be neutralized. Then part D gives us the basis for the dispute in parts A-B-C: If such a thing happens, you have to skim off the top layer. The reason is that the top layer is regarded as distinguishable from the rest, and it <u>is</u> possible to remove it to begin with, so the claim is that the <u>se'ah</u> which fell in is the one which is skimmed off. This is everyone's view, for R. Eliezer agrees one must remove the top layer -- that is the presupposition of B.

But Eliezer claims that if the top layer contains a hundred <u>se'ahs</u>, the Heave-offering is neutralized even in what has been skimmed off! Why must it be skimmed off? Because we do not know where the Heave-offering fell, or even whether it has been mixed up! Thus far according to Albeq and the traditional commentaries he relies upon.

However, let us consider the possibility that we have a composite pericope before us, one element of which is framed in terms of a dispute between Eliezer and Joshua, the other in terms of an anonymous, and unanimous rule:

Unanimous	Dispute
1. A <u>se'ah</u> of Heave-offering which fell on top of the store-jar	1. A <u>se'ah</u> of Heave-offering which fell on top of the store-jar
2. He should skim it off.	2. <u>And he skimmed it off</u>
3. --	3. R. Eliezer says, If in the skim is a hundred <u>se'ahs</u>, it is neutralized in a hundred and one.
4. --	4. R. Joshua says, It is not neutralized.

The final question supposedly pertains to both parts:

5.   If so, why have they said that Heave-offering neutralizes in a hundred and one?

For the unanimous version (D), the meaning is, Why should he have to skim off the top layer at all? And the answer is, one indeed does not have to skim off that layer, if the Heave-offering has been mixed up. Obviously, if one knows where the Heave-offering has fallen, he has no problems.

But the question when directed to parts B and C is strange. Eliezer says it is neutralized in a hundred and one. So he should not be asked why he does not say what he has just said. As to Joshua the question is a real question, but he never said a hundred and one parts will neutralize. For him, it is a hundred and a bit more. Now that may be a quibble, but it seems to me an important one, for Joshua cannot reasonably be asked to answer a question phrased in Eliezer's terms.

Now let us take no. 5 as an indication that something is wrong. If we look at no. 2 we see the problem: and he skimmed it off has contaminated A from D. Without it, we have also to remove the opening clause of B, If in the layer removed were... It no longer is pertinent to Eliezer's saying; the if-clause has been generated by he skimmed. Without the contaminating clause, what do we have?

A se'ah of Heave-offering which fell into the mouth of a store jar:
Eliezer: It is neutralized [in a hundred and one] (T'LH)
Joshua: It is not neutralized (L' T'LH)
This then is the same case as the foregoing, only in far simpler language. Just as Eliezer says the lower figs neutralize the upper ones, so he says the lower grain neutralizes the upper; and Joshua in both instances says the lower does not neutralize the upper.

The little series of "cases" therefore produces the following rules:

1.   Eliezer: One hundred and one.
      Joshua: One hundred and a bit more.
2.   Joshua: Black, large, round neutralize white, small, and square.
      Eliezer: No.
      Aqiba: If you know what fell into what, they do not [as in Eliezer's rule],
      but if you do not know, they do neutralize.

(This means we do not know whether black, large, or round has actually fallen into white, small, and square or not -- and Joshua's rule is now irrelevant.)

3.   Eliezer: Top neutralize bottom -- figs, wheat.
      Joshua: Top ones do not neutralize bottom.

As a matter of fact, Eliezer is consistent throughout. Where one really is not sure what has fallen into what, but the species are the same, then one thing will neutralize the other. And this then is consistent, in a general way, with Eliezer's position on Heave-offering for unclean from clean produce.

Why then has the glossator (M. Ter. 4:9-10) tried to show Eliezer "stringent" as well as "lenient"? I doubt that the glossator stands within the formative process of the pericopae. He simply comments on what he has before him. But in the case of M. Ter. 4:8-9, one wonders how closely he has looked, for, from Aqiba's viewpoint -- and he must be right -- there is no dispute between Joshua and Eliezer to begin with. Then the rearrangement of the names allows the more stringent position to come last, the less stringent one first -- according to the gloss, Joshua first, Eliezer second, then Eliezer first, and Joshua second. Since in M. Ter. 4:10 the opinions are not interchangeable but independent of one another, it was easy enough to rearrange things -- if that is what happened. However, since the form calls for (1) Eliezer (2) Joshua throughout, whoever is in the stringent position, it perhaps is M. Ter. 4:8A that has been rearranged to put Joshua first -- therefore, superficially, in Eliezer's position -- until Aqiba shows Eliezer's position to be normative, even in M. Ter. 4:8A. One obviously could not put 4:8B before A. One could, however, have Aqiba settle the matter so as to make A = B. My view is that 4:8A should have Eliezer to begin with. Joshua should prohibit, and we have no need for Aqiba at all.

A.   R. Eliezer says, "If he did not bring an instrument [for circumcision] before the Sabbath, he brings it openly on the Sabbath.

B.   "And in [time of] danger, he conceals it in the presence of witnesses."

C.   And further did R. Eliezer say, "They cut wood to make coals to make an iron instrument [for circumcision, on the Sabbath]."

D.   A general principle did R. Aqiba say, "Every kind of work which can be done before the Sabbath does not override the Sabbath, and which cannot be done before the Sabbath does override the Sabbath."

                                        M. Shabbat 19:1

Comment: Eliezer's rule should follow M. Shab. 19:2, which gives the general principle, "They may perform on the Sabbath all things that are needful for circumcision." Eliezer then deals with a detail of that rule -- carrying the knife.

By carrying the knife openly, the man shows that it is for the purpose of circumcision, which overrides the Sabbath. This will not accord with Aqiba's view that the work cannot be done before the Sabbath, so may be done on the Sabbath; Aqiba would rule that one brings the knife in advance. Eliezer's second rule is even more extreme. Certainly one can make the iron tool before the Sabbath. But Eliezer permits the work to be done even on the Sabbath. So the problem is not merely one of defining what can or cannot be done before the Sabbath, with both men in agreement. Eliezer does not say, if he did not cut wood/make fire, etc. His rule in C is unequivocal, They do so and so, without qualification. The if-clause of A may be harmonized with Aqiba's rule, but C cannot.

Albeck explains (Seder Mo'ed, p. 61), that Aqiba differs from Eliezer in respect to all things needed for the circumcision. Only the actual rite of circumcision overrides the Sabbath, but not preparation for that rite. This would place Eliezer in the lenient position, Aqiba in the strict.

B looks like a gloss added after the Bar Kokhba War. We have no evidence of a prohibition of circumcision during Eliezer's lifetime, and B, formally, bears no relationship to Eliezer's saying in A. A formal continuation of Eliezer's saying would have kept the same verb-form for openly and hidden, thus megulleh should be matched not by mekhassehu but by (ubassakkanah), mekhusseh. 'L PY 'DYM is a quibble.

Now as to 19:2: the general rule would seem to contradict Aqiba, to follow Eliezer, and to generalize Eliezer's principle:

A. R. Eliezer says, They do all the needs of the circumcision on the Sabbath --

B. Excision, tearing, sucking, and putting on a bandage, and cummin.

C. R. Aqiba says, Every kind of work which can be done...

The sayings are not closely balanced in form, but in substance they match one another. But then the examples (B) do not bear out Eliezer's rule. They impose distinctions which flow only from Aqiba's:

If this [cummin] had not been pounded upon the eve of the Sabbath, a man may chew it with his teeth and then apply it.

If the wine and oil had not been mixed on the eve of the Sabbath, each may be applied by itself.

They may not newly make the special bandage, but a rag may be wrapped around the member.

If this had not been prepared on the eve of the Sabbath, one may bring it wrapped around his finger even from another courtyard.

All of these rules accord with Aqiba's distinction between what may and may not be done in advance of the Sabbath. And they contradict the opening statement. But so too do the examples given in illustration of that statement. Excision and tearing are not the only "requirements" of the circumcision, so far as Eliezer is concerned. On the contrary, he even permits making a fire to heat coals to forge an iron knife! Excision, tearing, etc., do not illustrate all the needs of the circumcision. They so "qualify" all the needs as to reverse completely the meaning of the phrase! Now all the needs consist of, and specify, the actual act of circumcision, and that alone.

Eliezer's rules in A + C ought to have yielded 19:2, and perhaps they did. But then Aqiba's principle has generated a gloss that so changes the meaning of 19:2 as to render it an illustration of Aqiba's principle, instead of a statement of Eliezer's.

A.   These things in regard to the Passover override the Sabbath: (1) its slaughtering, and (2) tossing its bloods, and (3) scraping its entrails, and (4) burning its fat.

But (1) roasting it and (2) rinsing its entrails do not override the Sabbath.

B.   (3) Carrying it [to the Temple] and (4) bringing it from outside the Sabbath limit and (5) cutting off its wen [from the carcass -- compare b. Eruv. 103a] do not override the Sabbath.

C.   R. Eliezer says, "They override."

M. Pes. 6:1

A.   R. Eliezer said, "[Is it not logical:] If slaughtering, which is [biblically-prohibited] on account of work, overrides the Sabbath, these [aforementioned actions] which are [prohibited] on account of Shevut [= rabbinically-prohibited Sabbath-work], ought they not [also] override the Sabbath?"

B.   R. Joshua said to him, "The festival will prove the matter, on which they permitted [acts prohibited] on account of [biblically-specified] work but have prohibited on it [acts which are forbidden] on account of Shevut."

C.   R. Eliezer said to him, "What is the meaning of this, Joshua? What proof does a voluntary act (RSWT) [= cooking] afford with respect to a commandment [the Passover]?"

D.   R. Aqiba answered and said, "Sprinkling [the man made unclean by a corpse, on the third or seventh day] will prove the matter for it is a commandment, and it is [prohibited on the Sabbath] on account of Shevut, but does not override the Sabbath. So you, do not be astonished concerning these [aforementioned prohibitions], for, even though they are a commandment, they are [prohibited] on account of shevut, and they will not override the Sabbath."

E.   R. Eliezer said to him, "And concerning it [sprinkling itself] I argue: If slaughtering, which is [prohibited] on account of [biblical-forbidden Sabbath-] work overrides the Sabbath, sprinkling, which is [prohibited on the Sabbath] on account of Shevut [alone], is it not logical that it will override the Sabbath?"

F.   R. Aqiba said to him, "Or the opposite: If sprinkling, which is [prohibited on the Sabbath] on account of Shevut, does not override the Sabbath, slaughtering, which is [prohibited on the Sabbath] on account of [Sabbath] work, is it not logical that it should not override the Sabbath?"

G.   R. Eliezer said to him, "Aqiba, you have uprooted what is written in the Torah: Between the evenings in its appointed time [season] (Num. 9:3) -- whether on weekday or on the Sabbath."

H.   He said to him, "Master, bring me an Appointed time [season] for these [acts] such as the Appointed time for slaughtering."

I.   A general principle did R. Aqiba say, "Every kind of work which may be
done on Friday does not override the Sabbath. But slaughtering, which
cannot be done on Friday, does override the Sabbath."

M. Pes. 6:2

Comment: Had the Mishnah been formulated according to Eliezer's view, it would
have read simply, "Both slaughtering the Passover and its appurtenances (MKSYRYN)
override the Sabbath" -- against Aqiba's general rule, just as in M. Shab. 19:1, and as in M.
Pes. 6:2I. Eliezer would have held that everything concerned with the Passover sacrifice,
both before and afterward, may be done on the Sabbath, and this would include the
prohibitions (1) and (2) of M. Pes. 6:1A.

Just as Eliezer says the appurtenances of circumcision override the Sabbath (M.
Shab. 19:1-2), so he rules that every aspect of offering the Passover on the Sabbath, when
the fourteenth of Nisan coincides with that day, likewise overrides the Sabbath. The
antecedent rule lists four permitted actions, and five forbidden ones. Eliezer's saying in
C is simply, "They override." To what does he refer? A consists of two lists, These things
override. But these things do not override; then B has no topic-sentence, simply a
continuation of the list broken by the first do not override. Evidently the redactor
supposed all parties agree on prohibitions (1) and (2), and Eliezer differs on prohibitions
(3), (4), and (5). Prohibitions (1) and (2) are not immediately involved with the sacrifice,
rather with use of the animal thereafter; therefore they can wait until the end of the
Sabbath. Prohibitions (3), (4), and (5), on the other hand, relate to preparing for the
sacrifice. One cannot carry it out without bringing the sacrifice to the Temple, etc. So it
may be that the redactor is correct in assigning to Eliezer a lenient ruling only with
respect to prohibitions 3-5. But Tos. Pis. 5:1 explicitly alludes to what is done afterward.
The rule of Aqiba in M. Shab. 19:1 explains the opinion of A-B: "Any act of work that can
be done on Friday does not override the Sabbath, but what cannot be done on Friday
overrides the Sabbath." Only the actual slaughter and disposition of the carcass (tossing,
scraping, burning) are impossible to do except at the proper time on the Sabbath. While
we may distinguish, logically, between prohibitions (1) and (2), on the one side, and (3), (4),
and (5), on the other, if Eliezer is consistent with his view that one may even cut wood to
make charcoal to forge a knife for a Sabbath-circumcision, he probably would rule all five
are permitted, as in Tos. Pis. 5:1.

The rule on which all parties agree is that the actual slaughter of the Passover does
override the Sabbath. That rule is attributed to Hillel (Phar. I, pp. 231-235), but without
exception or qualification: They asked Hillel, Does the Passover override the Sabbath?
Accordingly, the issue is the sacrifice, without distinction as to the actions therein
involved. Eliezer's position places him closer to that assigned to Hillel than does Aqiba's
(below).

The pericope attached to the Hillel-story then raises the issue, "What will be the
rule for the people who did not bring knives and Passover-offerings to the sanctuary?"

This takes for granted that once the sacrifice itself is permitted, bringing the sacrifice to the Temple will still pose problems. To Hillel is assigned the answer, "He whose Passover was a lamb hid the knife in its wool, etc., so they brought knives and Passover-sacri- fices." That is, the lamb brought the knife. But who brought the lamb? Evidently the man himself did -- just as Eliezer rules in respect to "carrying it to the Temple and bringing it from outside the Sabbath limit." So the presupposition of the question follows the Aqiban viewpoint; the answer is Eliezer's -- but not really so, for he would have let the people carry the knives.

M. Pes. 6:2 supplies a complete set of arguments for Eliezer's position, introducing Joshua, then Aqiba! -- a composite. It looks to me as though we have two separate debates, A-C, Eliezer, Joshua, Eliezer, with Eliezer winning the argument, then D-H, Aqiba, Eliezer, Aqiba. But the division of the composite is obvious, for Aqiba's answer in D responds to Eliezer in A; only the extension of the original argument, Do not be astonished, links D to C. I is tacked on last of all, repeated from M. Shab. 19:1-2, or formulated according to the same theory of law. Since Aqiba is involved in M. Shab. 19:1-2, it seems that he, and not Joshua, should consistently give the contrary arguments here, as in Tos. Pis. 5:1.

In A Eliezer distinguishes between biblically- and rabbinically-prohibited actions in respect to the Sabbath. The former are more serious. Yet slaughtering is biblical- ly-prohibited on the Sabbath (except in the Temple) and is permitted with respect to the Passover-sacrifice. The carrying and bringing of the sacrifice, which are not 'work' in the biblical definition, but are prohibited merely by rabbinical rule, ought all the more to be permitted.

Joshua's reply must then show that the biblical prohibitions of Sabbath work are not invariably more strictly enforced than the rabbinical ones, so that the foregoing argument will not stand up. He points out that some biblically prohibited acts of work are permitted on the festival, while some rabbinically prohibited ones are prohibited. Joshua alludes to the rule in M. Bes. 5:2: "Any act culpable on the Sabbath, whether by virtue of rules concerning Sabbath rest (Shevut) or concerning acts of choice or concerning duties, is culpable also on a Festival-day... A festival day differs from the Sabbath only in respect to preparing necessary food." Preparing food involves prohibitions ordained in the Scriptures; these are permitted, but other actions, prohibited only by rabbinical rules on account of Shevut, are prohibited. Therefore, Joshua argues, the permission of a biblically-prohibited action, such as slaughtering, does not carry in its wake the per- mission of a rabbinically-prohibited one.

Eliezer in C introduces a further distinction, between a voluntary action (RSWT) and a commandment. In the latter, one has no choice but to do the deed. But one may or may not do other things. Eating is a voluntary action, not a commandment. But the command- ment involved in the Passover-sacrifice requires the violation of acts of Sabbath rest (Shevut). So Eliezer's second argument distinguishes preparation of food and sacrifice of the Passover. y. Pes. 6:2 supplies Eliezer with a further argument along the same lines.

Joshua would say, "The festal offering proves the matter, for they permitted doing 'work' for it but prohibited actions on account of Shevut." To this Eliezer would reply, "But punishment for not doing the festal offering properly does not involve cutting off, while punishment for not doing the Passover properly does involve cutting off."

In D, Aqiba reverts to the main issue introduced in A: Sprinkling the sin-offering water on one made unclean by reason of contact with a corpse on the third day of his becoming unclean (Num. 19:12) will be pertinent. If the seventh day occurs on the Sabbath which is also the eve of Passover, they do not sprinkle the unclean man, even in order that he may carry out the Passover, which is a commandment. Now the sprinkling is prohibited only on account of Shevut. Yet it does not override the Sabbath coinciding with Passover.

Strikingly, in this argument, Aqiba takes the rule for granted, yet, as we shall see, Eliezer rejects the law on which Aqiba's argument is based! This is a strange state of affairs. Normally in a debate all parties agree on the law, but differ as to its implications. A debate generally cannot be constructed between parties who do not agree on fundamental questions of fact.

In E, Eliezer argues about Aqiba's rule with respect to not sprinkling on the Passover that coincides with the Sabbath. So far as Eliezer is concerned, sprinkling the unclean man so that he can keep the Passover at the proper time is just as much an 'appurtenance' of the commandment as is the actual act of slaughter. If slaughtering is permitted, despite the biblical origin of its prohibition, sprinkling will likewise be permitted. So E refutes the facts, not the argument, of D.

Then, in F, Aqiba simply turns the argument around, again on the basis of a different view of the legal facts.

Eliezer introduces a scriptural proof -- the same one used by Hillel in Tos. Pis. 4:13 (Phar. I, p. 231)! Eliezer refers to the use of Its season with respect to the Passover (Num. 9:3), without developing the common occurrence into a heqqesh, as does Hillel. Its season here means that the Passover is carried out fully and completely when it is due, even on the Sabbath. Now to Eliezer this includes everything to do with the slaughtering, as he originally stated. But Aqiba's answer limits the probative value of Its season to the actual slaughtering. He says, Show me an Its season referring to the other actions which you would permit along with the slaughtering.

Then I makes clear the basic issue. Eliezer holds anything connected with the Passover is covered by Its season, while Aqiba holds only things which cannot be done on the Sabbath are protected by it.

I think it now is clear that the principles of the debate cover all seven items prohibited in 6:1A-B. Therefore A is formulated according to the Aqiban rule, and Eliezer's position as glossator is an Aqiban way of showing the decided law. The distinction between prohibitions (1) and (2), and (3)-(5) is of no consequence so far as the debate is concerned. But since the redactor has made such a distinction with the do not override, he has placed Eliezer in the position of agreeing with the Aqiban rule in 6:2I, contrary to the exact position made evident in 6:2A-H.

Where does Hillel fit in? Hillel's position in Tos. Pis. 4:13 is simply that the Passover-sacrifice <u>does</u> override the Sabbath. No distinctions are made in what aspects of the sacrifice do, and what do not, override the Sabbath -- and this is the position of Eliezer. Only after the general rule is established does Aqiba's distinction, between what can and cannot be done other than on the Sabbath, become significant. So Tos. Pis. (<u>Phar.</u> I, p. 231-2, that is, the whole of the debate on the general rule) seems to me consistent with Eliezer's position. The proof from <u>In its season</u> naturally is not attributed to Eliezer in the Hillel story, but Hillel's explicit use of <u>In its season</u> seems consistent with Eliezer's:

> "Another matter: It is said concerning the continual offering, <u>In its season</u> (Num. 28:2), and it is said concerning the Passover, <u>In its season</u> (Num. 9:2). Just as the continual offering, concerning which <u>In its season</u> is said, overrides the Sabbath, so the Passover, concerning which <u>In its season</u> is said, overrides the Sabbath."

Eliezer has a simpler argument based on <u>In its season</u>. The simple meaning of the clause is "whether on the weekday or on the Sabbath." Eliezer is not constrained to draw evidence from Num. 28:2, probably because the method of exegesis through <u>heqqesh</u> or similar analogical arguments was either unknown to him or unnecessary, I think the former.

It would therefore seem that Eliezer stands closer than does Aqiba to Hillel in Tos. Pis. 4:13. Aqiba inferentially accepts the basic issue confronted by Hillel -- whether one slaughters at all. Eliezer's denial of distinctions important to Aqiba but absent from the Hillel-story and his use of a central proof assigned to Hillel, seem to me to place Eliezer in the circle of thought attributed to Hillel -- if not in the House of Hillel. Or, to put it differently, the stories of Hillel's rise to power, focused as they are upon the issue of Sabbath/Passover, seem to draw upon materials shaped to begin with in the name of, and probably by, Eliezer.

A.   He who divorces his wife and says to her, "Lo, you are permitted to any man, except for so-and-so" --

B.   R. Eliezer permits.

C.   And sages prohibit.

D.   What should he do? He should take it from her and give it to her again and say, "Lo, you are free to marry any man."
     But if he had written [the condition in the <u>Get</u>], even if he erased it, the <u>Get</u> remains invalid.

M. Git. 9:1

<u>Comment</u>: Eliezer regards the conditional <u>Get</u> as valid. The wife may marry anyone except the specified man and is regarded as fully divorced. The sages say that she

is not divorced, since the husband has limited the force of the Get, which now does not permit her to marry anyone at all. D then depends upon, and takes for granted the correctness of the rule of, C.

A. He who divorces his wife and said to her, "Lo, you are permitted to any man except for so-and-so."

B. R. Eliezer permits her to marry any man except for that man.

C. And R. Eliezer agrees that if she remarried another and was widowed or divorced, she [then] is permitted to marry that one to whom she had been prohibited [by the exclusionary clause].

D. And after the death of R. Eliezer, four elders came together to reply to his opinions, R. Tarfon, R. Yosi the Galilean, R. Eleazar b. 'Azariah, and R. Aqiba. [y.+b. add: R. Joshua said to them, "Are you not answering the lion after death?"]

E. R. Tarfon said, "If she went and married his brother [of the one forbidden to her], and he died without issue, how is she going to enter Levirate marriage? Does it not result that he makes a [contractual] condition against [b.: Uproot] what is written in the Torah, and whoever makes a condition against what is written in the Torah -- his condition is invalid.
    "Thus we [Sifre: you] have learned that this is not 'cutting off.'"

F. R. Yosi the Galilean said, "Where have we found a forbidden connection ('RWH) in the Torah permitted to one [man] and prohibited to [another] one.
    "But she who is permitted to one is permitted to every man, and who is prohibited to one is prohibited to every man. Thus we have learned that this is not a 'cutting off.'"

G. R. Eleazar b. 'Azariah says, "Cutting off -- a thing [document] which cuts [the tie] between her and between him. [b.: Thus you have learned that this is not a 'cutting off']."

H. R. Yosi the Galilean said, "I prefer the words of R. Eleazar." [y. omits. b. has a separate baraita.]

I. R. Simeon b. Eleazar says, "If she went and married another, and he divorced her and said to her, 'Lo, you are permitted to every man' -- how does this one permit what the other had prohibited? Thus we have learned that this is not a 'cutting off.'"

J. R. Aqiba said [Sifre: says], "Lo, if the one to whom she was prohibited was a priest, and the one who divorced her died -- does it not come out that to him [that priest] she is a widow, but to [b.: everyone -- omits:] all his brothers, the priests, she is a divorcee!
    "Another matter [Sifre begins here]: And with whom did the Torah deal more stringently? Divorcées or widows? Divorcées are dealt with more

stringently than widows. Now the divorcée, who is more stringently treated, is not prohibited from the one who is prohibited, but a widow, who is less stringently dealt with -- is it not logical that she should be prohibited from him to whom she is permitted? [b.: There then follows an argument a fortiori: Seeing that she would have been forbidden to the priest as a divorcée, though this involves only a minor (transgression), should she not all the more as a married woman, which is much more serious, be forbidden to all men? From this you learn that this is no 'cutting off.']

"Another matter: She went and married another [b. From the market], and he had children from her and died [b.: She was widowed or divorced], when she returns to this one to whom she is [originally] prohibited, does it not come out that [b.: The Get is void] the children of the first are mamzerim? Thus you have learned that this is not a cutting off."

Tos. Git. 9:1-5

Comment: Deut. 24:1 speaks of a "book of cutting off," meaning a divorce-document which effects a "cutting off" or complete separation is required (b. Git. 21b).

C is necessary for the arguments of Tarfon and Aqiba that follow, which take for granted the inoperability of the clause after the first remarriage. Eleazar b. 'Azariah's and Yosi's arguments stand without reference to complications after the first remarriage. So C looks like an Aqiban interpolation.

The four surviving rabbis offer arguments against Eliezer's position that a conditional clause in a Get is acceptable. Tarfon points out the possibility that the Get contains a clause potentially contrary to Torah-law, for the husband cannot establish conditions which might make it impossible for the divorced wife to carry out the commandment concerning Levirate marriage. Yosi simply says that the divorce has to be complete. One cannot divorce for everyone, but remain married in respect to one man. Eleazar b. 'Azariah has essentially the same argument, but his is phrased in exegetical terms. Aqiba, like Tarfon, points out a possible anomaly in the situation. If the woman is prohibited from marrying a priest, and then the one who divorced her died, to that priest she now is not regarded as a divorcée -- if she were a divorcée, she could not marry him -- but only as a widow. So she cannot marry any priest except that one who was prohibited to her under the terms of the divorce. The qal vehomer spells out the anomaly.

Then comes a weightier argument. If later on she remarries and has children, and then the second husband dies, she may then marry the one prohibited in terms of the original divorce (as specified in C). But this act retroactively renders the children of the second marriage mamzerim, for their mother at the time of their birth was not legally divorced.

Eleazar b. 'Azariah's argument, based on exegesis, is selected by Rava and by Yosi. b.'s baraita, assigning the saying to Yosi b. Halafta, is probably better than Tos., which gives it to Yosi the Galilean, who is a party to the discussion.

Tos.'s text is satisfactory, because of the inclusion of the later Simeon b. Eleazar. Y. interpolates Amoraic comments. B. has straightened things out.

A. If it [the oven] was cut up into rings, and he put sand between each ring --

B. R. Eliezer declares clean.

C. And sages declare unclean.

D. This is the oven of 'Akhnai.

E. As for the cauldrons of the Arabs, which are hollows dug in the ground and plastered with clay, if the plastering can stand of itself, it is susceptible to uncleanness; otherwise it is not susceptible. Such was the oven of Ben Dinai.

M. Kel. 5:10

Comment: M. Kel. 5:8 states:

"If [the oven was cut up breadthwise into rings, so that each is less than four handbreadths high, it becomes insusceptible. If it was again set up and plastered over with clay, it becomes susceptible to uncleanness."

The oven before us has been cut into rings and then set up with sand. Eliezer declares it clean, because the sand intervenes between the rings and does not join them together. The sages declare it capable of receiving uncleanness, because the plastering over the sand joins the rings.

D alludes to the famous dispute in b. B.M. 59b. It looks like a gloss.

ii. Biographical Stories

A. We learnt elsewhere: If he cut it into separate tiles, placing sand between each tile, R. Eliezer declared [it] clean, and the sages declared it unclean; and this was the oven of 'Akhnai.

B. Why [the oven of] 'Akhnai? Said Rav Judah in Samuel's name, "[It means] that they encompassed it with arguments as a snake, and proved it unclean."

C. TN': On that day R. Eliezer brought forward all the arguments in the world, but they did not accept them.

D. (1) Said he to them, "If the law agrees with me, let this carob-tree prove it."

The carob-tree was torn a hundred cubits out of its place (others say four hundred cubits).

"No proof can be brought from a carob-tree," they said to him.

(2) Again he said to them, "If the law agrees with me, let the stream of water prove it." The stream of water flowed backwards.

"No proof can be brought from a stream of water," they said to him.

(3) Again he said to them, "If the law agrees with me, let the walls of the schoolhouse prove it." The walls inclined to fall.

R. Joshua rebuked them, saying, "When disciples of sages are engaged in a legal dispute, what have you to interfere?"

Hence they did not fall, in honor of R. Joshua, nor did they resume the upright, in honor of R. Eliezer. (And they are still standing thus inclined).

(4) Again he said to them, "If the law agrees with me, let it be proved from Heaven." An echo went forth and said, "Why do you dispute with R. Eliezer, seeing that in all matters the law agrees with him!"

But R. Joshua arose and exclaimed, "It is not in heaven (Deut. 30:12)."

D.   What did he mean by this? Said R. Jeremiah, "That the Torah had already been given at Mount Sinai; we pay no attention to an echo because Thou has long since written in the Torah at Mount Sinai, After the majority must one incline (Ex. 23:2)."

E.   R. Nathan met Elijah and asked him, "What did the Holy One, blessed be He, do in that hour?"

"He laughed [with joy]," he replied, "saying, 'My sons have defeated Me. My sons have defeated Me.'"

F.   It was said: On that day all objects which R. Eliezer had declared clean were brought and burnt in fire. Then they took a vote and excommunicated (BRK) him.

G.   Said they, "Who shall go and inform him?"

"I will go," answered R. Aqiba, "lest an unsuitable person go and inform him and thus destroy the whole world."

What did R. Aqiba do? He donned black garments and wrapped himself in black and sat at a distance of four cubits from him.

"Aqiba," said R. Eliezer to him, "why is today [different from] other days?"

"Master," he replied, "it appears to me that the fellows (HBRYM) hold aloof from you."

Therefore he too rent his garments, put off his shoes, removed [his seat] and sat on the earth, while tears streamed from his eyes.

H.   The world was then smitten: a third of the olive crop, a third of the wheat, and a third of the barley crop. Some say, the dough in women's hands swelled up.

I.   TN': Great was the calamity that befell that day, for everything at which R. Eliezer cast his eyes was burned up.

J.   R. Gamaliel too was travelling in a ship, when a huge wave arose to drown him.

"It appears to me," he said, "that this is on account of none other than R. Eliezer b. Hyrcanus."

Thereupon he arose and exclaimed, "Sovereign of the Universe! Thou knowest full well that I have not acted for my honor, nor for the honor of my paternal house, but for Thine, so that strife may not multiply in Israel!"

At that the raging sea subsided.

K.   [What follows is in Aramaic:] Imma Shalom was R. Eliezer's wife, and sister of R. Gamaliel. From the time of this incident onwards she did not permit him to fall upon his face [in supplication].

Now a certain day happened to be New Moon, but she mistook a full month for a defective one.

Others say, a poor man came and stood at the door, and she took out some bread to him. [On her return] she found him fallen on his face.

"Arise," she cried out to him, "you have slain my brother."

In the meanwhile an announcement (SYPWR') was made from the house of Rabban Gamaliel that he had died. "How do you know it?" he questioned her.

"I have this tradition from my father's house: All gates are locked, excepting the gates of wounded feelings."

L.   TNW RBNN: He who wounds the feelings of a proselyte transgresses three negative injunctions, and he who oppresses him infringes two. Wherein does wronging differ? Because three negative injunctions are stated: Viz. Thou shall not wrong a stranger [i.e. a proselyte] (Ex. 22:20). And if a stranger sojourn with three in your land, he shall not wrong him (Lev. 19:33). And ye shall not therefore wrong each his fellowman (Lev. 25:17), a proselyte being included in 'fellowman'. But for oppression also three are written, viz., and thou shall not oppress him (Ex. 22:20). Also thou shalt not oppress a stranger (Ex. 23:9), and [If thou lend money to any of my people that is poor by thee,] thou shalt not be to him as a usurer (Ex. 22:24) which includes a proselyte! But [say] both [are forbidden] by three [injunctions].

M.   TNY': R. Eliezer the Great said, "Why did the Torah warn against [the wronging of] a proselyte in thirty-six (or as others say, in forty-six) places? Because he has a strong inclination to evil."

b.   B.M.   59a-b,   trans.   H.
Freedman, pp. 352-355

A.   They sought to excommunicate R. Liezer.

They said, "Who will go and inform him?"

R. Aqiba said, "I shall go and inform him."

He came to him.

He said to him, "Rabbi, see, your colleagues (HBRYK) are excommunicating you (MNDYN LK)."

B. He [Eliezer] took him and went outside. He said, "O carob, carob, if the law is like their words, uproot yourself," and it did not uproot itself.

"If the law is according to my words, uproot yourself," and it uprooted itself.

"If the law is like their words, return [to your place]," and it did not return.

"If the law is like my words, return to your place," and it returned.

C. All such praise and the law is not according to R. Eliezer?

R. Hanina said, "Once it has been given out, it has been given only on condition that one follows the majority, even in error."

And does R. Eliezer not accept the principle that one follows the majority even in error?

He paid no attention until in his very presence they burned the things he had declared clean.

D. There we have learned (TMN TNYNN): If he broke it into rings and put sand between the rings --

R. Liezer declares clean.

And sages declare unclean.

This is the oven of 'Akhnai.

E. R. Jeremiah said, "A great tribulation (HKK) took place [Lit.: it was made] on that day. Wherever R. Liezer's eye looked, it was burned, and not only so, but even one grain of wheat -- the half [that he looked at] would be burned, and [the other] half not burned."

F. And the columns of the assembly-house were shaking.

R. Joshua said to them, "If the fellows (HBRYM) are contending, what business is it of yours?"

F. And an echo came forth and said, "The law follows Eliezer, my son."

R. Joshua said, "It is not in heaven."

G. R. Qerispai, R. Yohanan in the name of Rabbi, "If a man should say to me, 'Thus did R. Liezer teach,' I should teach according to his words, but (DTNY') the Tannas exchange [the teachings of Eliezer are not attributed to him accurately]."

H. One time he was going through the market and he saw one woman cleaning her house, and she threw out [the dirt], and it fell on his head.

He said, "It would seem that today my colleagues will bring me near, as it is written, From the dung heap he will raise up the poor (Ps. 113:7)."

Y. M.Q. 3:1

Comment: The version of y. M.Q. is disjointed and out of order. These are the fragments of a story before they have been put together into a smooth and coherent account.

A begins with a reference to the excommunication of Eliezer, but it supplies no reason for that action. This only comes later. The story flows into B. Aqiba tells Eliezer he is being excommunicated. Eliezer presumably knows the reason -- but the oven of 'Akhnai is not mentioned -- and then calls upon nature to support his opinion. Nature obliges, in the form of the carobs. b. greatly expands this segment of the story. C then gives discussion of the foregoing. Why does Eliezer differ from the majority? C ends with the reference to burning Eliezer's 'purities.' D then brings in the oven of 'Akhnai; it should have come at the outset, or at least as an introduction to B. b. puts it into its logical place.

Jeremiah's story about Eliezer's magical power is now a fragment, to be developed in b.

F then alludes to the (evidently famous) trembling walls, which supplies the occasion for Joshua's rebuke, and then the second, and similar chria follows. Heaven announces Eliezer is right, and Joshua says the Torah is not in heaven.

Finally we have Yohanan's striking citation of Rabbi [Judah the Patriarch] that the law should normally follow Eliezer, but the Tannaitic tradents suppress his name or give his teachings to others. Finally it tells a little story, which shows that Eliezer was disheartened by his experience -- to his credit.

These bits and pieces are, as noted, out of proper sequence. They suggest that a terminus post quem for the story should be about the time of Rabbi Judah the Patriarch. M. Kel. 5:10 alludes to the "famous" oven, so presumably some story (or stories) about the oven of 'Akhnai circulated before the time of the Mishnah's compilation or the interpolation of "oven -- 'Akhnai". But precisely what they consisted of is difficult to say. The duplicated chria of Joshua's rebuking nature/heaven cannot give evidence of a pre-Mishnaic version, nor does the saying of Hanina. A better terminus is probably Jeremiah, who tells in his own name a story later on fully articulated by the authority of a Tanna.

b. B.M. shows us what a baraita-editor could do with such materials. First of all, everything is set in logical order. The complex pericope begins with an allusion to M. Kel. 5:10, then the story, beginning in C, unfolds. Eliezer offers numerous proofs, but none is accepted. Then the carob tree is brought in; it is not merely uprooted, but torn a hundred cubits out of place. This is then duplicated: a stream of water flows backward. Then the walls of the school-house are introduced to complete a triad of action. Now comes, as the climax, the heavenly voice. The y. M.Q. allegation that the law follows Eliezer is expanded: now heaven says the law always follows him. Joshua cites the appropriate Scripture.

E is introduced quite separately. Why Nathan should be chosen to deliver Elijah's message I cannot say; but Nathan supplies no terminus for the story.

F then rejoins the original story. Since Eliezer has been rejected by the sages, what he regards as clean is burned. Only then is Eliezer excommunicated -- probably the beginning of the whole assemblage.

Now, in G, comes the problem of informing him. Since Eliezer's mastery of nature is an issue, it is important that he be told such in a way that he will not be moved to destroy the world. So Jeremiah's story in y. M.Q. is not only revised, but expanded and duplicated. But it would seem to me some such consideration lies behind G's story. Now Eliezer's reaction is not to call on nature for proof, as in y. M.Q., but to accept his excommunication. But then H tells us that nature did punish the excommunication of Eliezer. This should not have been included, for Eliezer's reaction in b. B.M. G is sufficient: he wept. Then, to make matters worse, b. B.M. I repeats H. Jeremiah is dropped.

I also serves to introduce J, but it is a bad introduction, since Gamaliel's experience has nothing to do with fire. Gamaliel is allowed to say that the issue was keeping the peace, so heaven should forbear. No one evidently is bothered by the problem of how Gamaliel, who supposedly was at the consistory, got out to sea. It is a formulary cliché to have Gamaliel on a boat. I suppose it seemed natural to include the tidal wave, but this is a bad setting for a good saying.

K then develops the theme that Eliezer could have destroyed the world. Imma Shalom kept Eliezer from 'falling on his face,' that is, from offering his individual supplication to God (Tahanun). God would listen and punished Gamaliel her brother. The occasion on which she slipped up is confused. The New Moon case is this: She thought the thirtieth of the month would be the New Moon, on which private prayers are not said, so she relaxed her watch. But the thirtieth was not the New Moon, so he said the supplications. Or, alternatively, a poor man came and she relaxed her watch on her husband; he then said the supplication. At any rate, she miraculously knew that her brother had died. So Eliezer's prayers killed him. This is turned into a case of knowing from a distance that a supernatural event has taken place. But even this supernatural skill is forthwith rationalized. She knew it not because she was confident of her husband's supernatural power, but because of a teaching that the prayers of anyone -- not only of a holy man -- whose feelings had been hurt would be listened to in heaven.

L. then goes on to another matter, namely, hurting the feelings of a proselyte; it is included because M has Eliezer's saying that the Scriptures have given strong protection to the proselyte. L-M have nothing to do with the foregoing stories, but are connected by the two themes: Eliezer and hurt feelings.

A.   M'SH B: R. Eliezer was seized on account of matters of Minut, and they
       brought him up before the court (BMH) for judgment.
       That hegemon said to him, "Should an elder like you involve [himself] in
       these matters?
       He said to him, "The judge (DYYN) is faithful for me (N'MN 'LY) [= "I
       rely upon the Judge."]
       That hegemon thought that he spoke only of him [himself], but he meant
       only his Father who is in heaven.

He said to him, "Since you have relied upon me, so have I said, "Is it possible that these white hairs should err (HSYBWT HLLW TW'YM) in such matters? Dismissus [= Pardoned (DYMWS)]. Lo, you are free."

B.   And when he had left the court (BMH), he was upset that he was seized on account of matters of Minut.

His disciples came in to comfort him and he would not accept [comfort].

R. Aqiba entered and said to him, "Rabbi, May I say something before you? Perhaps you will not be distressed."

He said to him, "Speak."

He said to him, "Perhaps one of the Minim said something to you of Minut and gave you benefit (WHN'K).

C.   He said, "By heaven! You have reminded me. One time I was walking in the camp ('YSTRTY') of Sepphoris. I found Jacob of Kefar Sikhnin, and he said something of Minut in the name of Jesus b. Pantiri [Alt.: PNDYR'] and gave me benefit (NH'NY), and I was seized on account of matters of Minut, for I transgressed teachings of Torah: Keep your way far from her and do not go near the door of her house... (Prov. 5:8)."

D.   R. Eliezer would say, "A man should always flee from what is ugly and from what looks like something ugly."

The pericope is in three parts. First (A) is the story of the trial. Eliezer outwits the judge by saying something intended for Heaven, which the judge took to be intended for himself. B ties the foregoing to a related, but separate account, (C), of Eliezer and the Minim, which is intended to illustrate that one must have no benefit whatever from, or relationships with, Minim. D then formulates an appropriate apodictic saying to conclude the second story.

CHAPTER TWO
SORTING OUT THE TRADITIONS

Sorting out the traditions about Eliezer ben Hyrcanus is made possible by a simple fact. We have comments in the names of later masters about things attributed to him. Some of these masters are assumed to have lived in the period between 70 and 130, during which the center of sages' activity was in Yavneh. We assign to Yavnean times, therefore, materials involving Eliezer on which named masters of that period make observations. Other materials bear observations or interpolations of various sorts in the names of authorities who flourished from 130 to 170, at the time at which the center of sages' work was at a Galilean town called Usha. These Ushan observations mark off yet a second layer in the unfolding tradition. Still other materials bear the attestation provided only by the document in which they first occur. That is to say while a statement attributed to Eliezer that bears no marks of comments by someone who lived between his time and the redaction of the Mishnah certainly was known by the time of the Mishnah, we cannot show that that statement was known before the Mishnah's publication. Hence the Mishnah itself attests to the availability of the saying at hand. The same judgment pertains to sayings that first occur in still later rabbinic documents, such as the Tosefta, the Fathers according to R. Nathan, two Talmuds, the compilations of scriptural exegeses, such as Sifra, Genesis Rabbah and Leviticus Rabbah. On this basis we may develop sound criteria for the evaluation of the relative usefulness of various traditions about Eliezer b. Hyrcanus.

We must regard as the "best" traditions, and probably reliable reports, materials for which we have chains of tradition and Yavnean attestations. The reason is that, concerning such materials, we know how a tradition was framed and handed on. We therefore can assess the possible presence of special interests or tendencies which may have affected its formation and transmission. We have reason to claim the responsible authority should have known what he was talking about. And we stand very close to the person of Eliezer himself. A tradition attested at Yavneh on the face of it should be dependable, for Eliezer himself is supposed to have lived through much of the Yavnean period -- to about 90 at the least -- and therefore should have exerted some control over the formulation and transmission of sayings he originally produced. The larger numbers of such sayings, moreover, come down in the names of, or are attested by, masters alleged to have been Eliezer's own students and colleagues. We therefore are on firm ground in postulating that the master has been accurately represented by authorities who knew what they were talking about on the basis of direct, first-hand experience. The traditions attested at Yavneh and with Yavnean chains of traditions therefore constitute the most reliable corpus of materials, against which all others are to be tested.

Even the best traditions, however, cannot be regarded as stenographic reports of what Eliezer actually said. Indeed, it is difficult to imagine that a report consisting of

One does not give Heave-offering for the unclean from the clean. R. Eliezer says, "One gives Heave-offering from the clean for the unclean..."

begins in a little dialogue, in which one master, or an anonymous chorus of masters, states the first line, and Eliezer, in the solo part, pronounces the second. Whatever Eliezer originally taught has been reworked for inclusion in an objective and neutral framework of laws, organized along logical and orderly lines, independent of Eliezer's own agendum, viewpoint, and circle of disciples. At some point before the Bar Kokhba War, however, something very like the opinion of Eliezer must have been stated in his name, for later masters in the middle or late period of Yavneh's history evidently knew both the anonymous opinion and Eliezer's. We cannot be sure that they knew these opinions in the exact form and wording now before us. But for our purposes, it is sufficient to be able to show that Eliezer held such an opinion. It is important to know whether he said it in the words before us only if we propose a close exegesis not of the legal theme, but of the language of the opinion in the very formulation now at hand; and this, while desirable, is not necessary for our limited historical-biographical purposes. In claiming that Yavnean traditions attested at Yavneh, with or without sound chains of transmission, are relatively reliable testimonies, I thus suggest that what is reliable is the substance of the opinion attributed to Eliezer. As to both the form in which it occurs and the exact wording, we as yet are able to say nothing.

This, however, means that even the best traditions about Eliezer -- and these certainly are better than the preserved traditions about pre-70 masters, the Houses, or Yohanan b. Zakkai -- are not so good as we might hope. They are not traditions to which Eliezer has given final form; they are not autobiographical; they are not in exactly Eliezer's language; and they were not finally redacted under the ultimate control of Eliezer himself. Others in his own time and for a long while thereafter had a share in the redaction of even these traditions. But from the viewpoint of the history of the rabbinic tradition, these are the first comparatively useful historical materials about an individual master.

One cannot compare their historical usefulness, however, to that of the sorts of traditions a man might produce for and about himself. For all his limitations, Josephus, for example, has given us the record of his own view of things in pretty much his own language. That record seems not to have undergone a process of transmission, and therefore revision and 'improvement,' for hundreds of years before it reached the form now before us. Nor did the opinion of Josephus carry preponderant weight, so as to form the basis for appeal to 'ancient authorities.' This fact generally preserved Josephus from the fabrications of the pious of later times, since, apart from the alleged Christian interpolations, no one had any practical interest in counterfeiting in his name stories made up only later on. But since, like all the other Tannaitic masters, Eliezer's opinion was authoritative long after he died -- if only to assure acceptance of the opposite view -- it was in some measure normal for a later master, or tradent, or even a scribe, to add a negative, or to switch Eliezer's opinion with that of the majority, or to give in Eliezer's name the opinion of his opponent -- and in later Tannaitic and early Amoraic times, these things certainly were done. We know of a few instances. We do not know in how many more Eliezer's words have been subjected to the improvement of people with a vested interest in having him say something other than what he or his disciples had originally handed on.

The best traditions, therefore, are excellent primarily by comparison with traditions first attested later on, at Usha, and those lacking a chain of tradition. These we may regard as "better" traditions. They are better than materials attested later on or not at all because they find attestations in comments of masters who were taught by Yavneans. In Eliezer's case, moreover, the Ushan masters ought to have had accurate information, for they had studied with Aqiba -- so we are told -- and therefore had direct access, if primarily through him, to Joshua's and Eliezer's teachings. We may take seriously the thematic agenda of laws of earlier figures attested by the Ushans, but we should find it difficult to accept the exact definitions of those disputes and decided laws. If the Ushans tended to refine the legal disputes of earlier figures it probably was because they had before them a statement of those disputes in a grosser form, concerning a more funda- mental question, than later seemed appropriate for debate. But with Eliezer the Ushans ought to have done less by way of revision of the received materials, because of the information coming from Aqiba himself, on the other. These attestations ought, therefore, to be more reliable than the Ushan ones for the Houses' pericopae.

The fair traditions are those attested at Bet Shearim, in the circle of masters around Judah the Patriarch who sponsored the Mishnah. That they might uncover reliable Eliezer-traditions unknown for a century seems unlikely, but not impossible; we cannot claim that the formulation and redaction of the traditions from Yavneh, and even Usha, proceeded in so thorough, systematic, and orderly a way as to leave out nothing and to include everything authentic.

What first surfaces in Mishnah-Tosefta, as I said at the outset, cannot be dismissed, but so far as possible, must be measured against the contents of materials already well-attested before then. Before a more detailed picture of the formation of Mish- nah-Tosefta and of the ways in which earlier materials were preserved until inserted in that compilation is available, however, we can offer no very firm opinion on the usefulness of such material as first occurs there. That few chains of tradition extend from Yavneh through the Mishnah seems to me an important limitation on the credibility of materials first known in Mishnah-Tosefta.

CHAPTER THREE
THE BEST TRADITIONS

i. Yavnean Attestations

We assume that if a later Yavnean master gives evidence of having known a teaching in the name of Eliezer, then that teaching in Eliezer's name may be presumed to have been in existence, in substance if not in the exact form and language now before us, before the time of said master. But in so assuming, do we not take for granted in the case of the later Yavnean what we deny to Eliezer, namely, that the saying attributed to the master in question has actually been said by him? Having denied a mere allegation that Eliezer made a statement is to be taken for granted, we thus seem to accept at face value the allegation that someone after Eliezer has made a statement with respect to Eliezer and his opinions. Furthermore, in regard to the Houses' traditions, we likewise assume that if a statement is attributed to Eliezer about a dispute between the Houses of Shammai and Hillel, the dispute between the Houses comes before Eliezer's time. He knew the dispute, it has been claimed, in pretty much its present formulation, and commented on it. So as we proceed from the earliest strata to the later ones, we seem to postpone the inevitable problem of the veracity of both attributions and what is attributed, taking for granted when studying the former generations the validity of sayings attributed to their successors, then bringing into doubt those very sayings as we proceed to examine the traditions attributed to the successors themselves. Why take at face value what is attributed to Eliezer in reference to the Houses but raise questions about sayings attributed to Eliezer in reference to issues evidently current in his own time or subjects untreated by antecedent authorities?

The answer lies in the original definition of attestations (Rabbinic Traditions About the Pharisees Before 70 [=Phar.] [Leiden, 1971: E.J. Brill], pp. 180-184): By attestation is meant the effort to find a terminus ante quem for a pericope in some evidence outside the structure of the pericope itself. If a saying is attributed to a later master concerning a pericope, but the master evidently stands outside of the pericope, we suppose that the issue or opinion given in the pericope was known to him. That assumption is based upon the principle that, if a saying is attributed to a master, he supplies a firm terminus a quo for the saying. Within the rabbinic circles no one earlier was likely to have said it, if the substance of the saying begins with him, for such a claim of priority simply is not made in respect to that saying by the rabbinic tradents later on. Obviously, it was common enough pseudepigraphically and anachronistically to attribute to an early authority and opinion formulated only after on, so as to gain greater credence for the opinion. But we need not claim more than did the pseudepigraphs themselves. If they were willing to go to an early Yavnean authority but not to Simeon the Just or Hillel, then we hardly are justified in reading the saying in anything like its present form back into Simeon's or Hillel's time. The pseudepigraphs thus supply a limit to the possible anachronisms to be taken into account.

When, moreover, we suppose Eliezer supplies an attestation for a dispute between the Houses, we claim only that that dispute was known in Yavnean times. In Phar. III, pp. 199-209, 223-231, we treated Yavnean attestations as a group, for our claim was only that what evidently was known to Yavneans may as a whole be taken to represent the state of the Houses' tradition by the end of the Yavnean period. Our stress was on the themes of the allegedly attested pericopae, not on their specific wording or rulings. We did not take for granted more than that a saying attributed to Eliezer glossing a Houses' dispute did not come before the time of Eliezer. Unless shown otherwise, we further supposed the Houses' dispute was not formulated all at once so as to include Eliezer's gloss. It was, after all, commonplace to include Yavneans (e.g., Aqiba) within the structure of Houses' dispute and therefore unnecessary to construct pericopae in such a way as to leave the Yavneans solely in the position of mere commentators or glossators -- unless that is exactly what they were.

For detailed information we never relied on a single pericope with its attestation or on the attestations of a single master. What we found were remarkable thematic consistencies among the attestations of the several Yavnean masters. Taken together, they seemed to show that the Yavneans had in hand Houses' materials in a narrowly-circumscribed range of subjects: agricultural tithes, offerings and taboos; uncleanness laws; and Sabbath and festival laws (Phar. III, p. 227). Because the sayings attributed to a large number of individual Yavnean masters seemed to reflect knowledge of much the same agendum, it seemed likely that the Yavneans as a group knew about Houses' materials appropriate to that agendum. That was our sole claim about the substance of the Houses' pericopae in Yavnean times. It also seemed likely that the Houses' form was known to Yavneans, for practically everyone at Yavneh knew pericopae in that form. So what we have taken at face value is only attributions of sayings about given subjects to particular Yavnean masters, not the veracity in detail of all that is attributed. Our view therefore is that if to the more important Yavneans is attributed knowledge of the Houses' dispute-form, that form probably comes no later than those Yavneans. If, likewise, many Yavneans are supposed to have known about Houses' rulings on a certain, limited legal agendum, then those rulings are apt to come no later than the group of Yavneans to which the sayings are attributed. We are very far indeed from taking at face value pretty much everything attriubuted to the early Yavneans about the Houses' disputes.

All we have really postulated is that the several masters' materials were not pseudepigraphically produced all at once, in a single circle, by the same hand, when Mishnah-Tosefta was compiled, that is, long after the period in question. We have supposed that those materials were produced in various places, times, and circles, by differing authorities, some of them nearer, others farther, from the period of the masters themselves. When, therefore, we notice important points in common among discrete sources, we legitimately suppose that those points in common are to be taken -- in a general way -- as testimony about the state of affairs prevailing at the very latest by the middle or latter part of the Yavnean period.

Yavnean attestations of Eliezer's traditions likewise cannot be taken to mean that the traditions were, individually and in detail, in their present form by the end of the Yavnean period and generally known to Yavnean masters. We therefore do not take at face value what Yavneans other than, and after, Eliezer were supposed to have said, while calling into question what Eliezer himself is alleged to have taught. We seek a picture of what several individuals or circles of disciples in different places and at different times in the Yavnean period seem to have known in regard to Eliezer. We do take for granted that those several individuals were not in collusion but approached the Eliezer-materials from varying perspectives; further, that the traditions of the several individuals were handed on in different ways to different circles. Hence points of agreement among the various authorities ought to suggest a few reliable generalities about the state of opinion about Eliezer before ca. A.D. 120.

ii. Two Examples of the Best Traditions

Tos. Ter. 3:18/M. Ter. 2:1 and Tos. Hal. 1:10/M. Hal. 2:8 concern a fundamental principle in the giving of Heave-offering. The anonymous rule states that one does not give Heave-offering from what is clean for what is unclean, but if one has done so, the Heave-offering is acceptable. Eliezer holds a still more lenient view, that one may do so in the first place. Likewise, Eliezer says one may take clean Dough-offering for the unclean. Eliezer obviously will accept the principle that one may not give from worse for better produce, hence unclean for clean; otherwise people would routinely give the poorer for the better. But the whole complex of rules about not giving Heave-offering from one variety of produce for some other variety of produce here finds its first major exception. Eliezer's ruling, if brought to its logical conclusion, ought to have loosened up other rules as well and in later stages of development to have allowed the giving of Heave-offering from grapes for wine, or from raisins for grapes. In M.Ter. 1:4 we have a Houses' dispute about giving Heave-offering from olives for oil or grapes for wine. One does not do so. If one has done so, the House of Shammai say, "It may still be deemed Heave-offering for the olives or grapes themselves" -- but not for the wine. Eliezer does not rule on that question, but in allowing an exception in the rigid rules, he might, as observed, have come to such a conclusion. At any rate he is in a lenient position vis à vis the anonymous rule, as is the House of Shammai vis à vis the House of Hillel.

Tos. Ter. 3:18 provides a chain of tradition for M. Ter. 2:1. Ilai here quotes Eliezer in exactly the language given in M. Ter. in Eliezer's name without Ilai's attestation. He further explains that in Eliezer's opinion dry (therefore, clean) produce may be given as Heave-offering even if it is not nearby.

Tos. Ter. 3:16 has Eliezer supply a Houses' dispute on a related issue. If a man gave Heave-offering of grapes intended for eating but then made the grapes into raisins, it is Heave-offering -- even though this produce whose preparation has been eventually completed serves as Heave-offering for produce whose preparation has not been completed, for one does not have to give Heave-offering a second time. Eliezer says the House of Shammai say one does not have to give Heave-offering a second time -- the anonymous ruling -- and the House of Hillel say one does have to give Heave-offering a second time.

I can imagine no reason for Ilai to have invented in Eliezer's name so novel a position. It is possible, to be sure, that Ilai had to attribute to his master a position he himself originated, so as to secure acceptance of his own opinion. But in Tos. Ter. 3:16 Eliezer himself is alleged to have given as a dispute between the Houses, with the House of Shammai in a position congruent to his own, what was also known as an undisputed law. M. Ter. 1:4 has the dispute in Eliezer's version -- that is, as an argument between the Houses -- but Eliezer is not cited as formulator of the dispute.

Accordingly, three versions of the matter existed: (1) An anonymous, unanimous statement of the law in accord with the opinion attributed by Eliezer to the House of Shammai; (2) Eliezer's statement that the matter is disputed by the Houses; (3) the representation of the matter as disputed by the Houses without Elizer's allegation to that effect. Now one fact seems sure: after ca. 100-120 A.D. a master who wanted his ideas to be accepted would attribute them to the House of Hillel or to a unanimous rabbinical consensus. By the Bar Kokhba War the tendency of rabbinic circles, particularly under Aqiban leadership, was to favor the opinion of the House of Hillel. With the reconstitution of the rabbinical authority at Usha it was perfectly clear that the law would follow the opinion of the House of Hillel. So we have no reason whatever to suppose a post-120 master would attribute to the House of Shammai an opinion he wished to have accepted. Yet Eliezer is supposed -- by Ilai's testimony -- to have taken a position roughly congruent to that of the Shammaites, and he is supposed -- by Tos. Ter. 3:16A -- to have claimed that what someone knew as a unanimous opinion was in fact only that of the House of Shammai. I see two possible explanations. Either he agreed with the opinion and attributed the dispute to the Houses and his own view to the House of Shammai, because the pericope was early and a Shammaite attribution would strengthen the possibility of acceptance of his view. Or a later master wished to set aside the testimony of an anonymous, unanimous law, with which he in fact differed, and therefore put into Eliezer's mouth the allegation that the law was the opinion of the House of Shammai and disputed by the House of Hillel. Doing so at once set aside the authority of the anonymous version and called into question the acceptability of its (=the House of Shammai's) opinion. Since Eliezer was (later on) taken to be a Shammaite, he would be expected to know the facts of the matter. In that case the Tos. Ter. 3:16B-evidence would derive from a period long after Yavneh. Between these two possibilities, the evidence of Ilai seems to me to favor the former. It was Eliezer's real opinion. Ilai knew it with respect to the problem of Heave-offering and attributed it to Eliezer because he had learned it from Eliezer.

Conditional Divorce

In M. Git. 9:1 Eliezer rules that a conditional writ of divorce is valid. The ruling is attested by Yosi b. R. Judah, so b. Git. 82a-b. Tos. Git. 9:1-5 has a story about how, after Eliezer had died, Tarfon, Yosi, Eleazar b. Azariah, and Aqiba met to refute the position of Eliezer. The y. and b. versions add that Joshua reproved them. The story itself draws together four proofs for the view contrary to Eliezer's. But the proofs are not equally valid and also tend to repeat one another. Yosi is repeated by Eleazar, Tarfon and Aqiba have essentially the same argument. So merely in order to state -- in dramatic form -- four separate objections to Eliezer's view it was unnecessary to invent such a story. It turns out in later rabbinic opinion that Eleazar b. Azariah's is best. Aqiba's circle therefore is not the likely source of the story.

How valid an attestation do we have in this story? The story itself is not attested before the third century. It follows standard rabbinic form: four opinions expressed in a dramatic setting, thus a well-developed chria. The story-line of the tale consists of the introductory clause, that Eliezer had died, and the sages got together to refute his opinion -- not an uncommon motif in Yavnean materials. But the sages, all middle- and later-Yavneans, are taken to be specific, differentiated individuals -- a sign of authenticity. At the very least the story should indicate that the circles of disciples around four masters registered an opinion different from Eliezer's. But it also strongly suggests that the masters or their circles independently knew and rejected Eliezer's position. The assemblage of the four ought further to reflect a fairly wide-spread opposition to Eliezer. Other stories of Eliezer's death and legal issues introduced in that connection know nothing of the conditional divorce. Some of the same masters are involved in these stories -- Eleazar b. Azariah and Aqiba in particular, Joshua as well. From the tendency to link the death of Eliezer to legal issues I learn that a tendency of story-tellers -- whether Yavnean or otherwise we cannot say -- was to ask whether controversial opinions of Eliezer had ultimately been retracted by him, and whether his associates and their associates had refuted them.

Clearly, Eliezer's approval of a conditional writ of divorce represents a most controversial opinion. It is lenient in the extreme to allow a divorce to take effect if a woman is allowed by the husband to marry almost anyone else; the exclusion in no way is supposed to impair the force of the document. Divorce is all the easier; the husband may have revenge on a wife he conceives, without firm evidence, to have been unfaithful, even though he has no better recourse. Eliezer surely is consistent with the very lenient attitude of the House of Hillel (Phar. II, pp. 37-39) and with the position attributed to Aqiba in the same pericope. Eliezer's opinion here is consistent also with his strict position in M. Sot. 1:1: a husband, having warned his wife before two witnesses, may make her undergo the rite of the suspected adulteress merely on the basis of his own evidence. And his opinion in M. Sot. 6:1 is equally relevant; virtually any sort of evidence at all is acceptable. All this accords with his view, M. Sot. 3:4, that a man should not allow his daughter to study the Torah. While not conclusive, it is highly suggestive that a number of opinions of Eliezer on quite separate issues reveals an entirely consistent position, in favor of a man's rights over a woman's. Perhaps Eliezer's consistency in the matter led him to the extreme view attributed to him in M. Git. 9:1.

iii. The Earliest Eliezer

Eliezer's rulings sometimes contain general principles; either he states such a principle, along with diverse applications, or he rules in such a way as to produce out of specific cases a general law. This seems to be an innovation, for to the earlier masters, the Houses, and Yohanan b. Zakkai are attributed few, if any, generalizations; rules assigned to the former generations apply to discrete cases. Perhaps Eliezer attempted to legislate according to a coherent philosophy, but we have only a little evidence to suggest so.

While we have some evidence of hostility toward Eliezer, few of the best traditions -- such as Ilai's and Aqiba's lists -- give us information on the grounds for such hostility or contain expressions of a negative view of Eliezer's teachings, as in Ishmael's story. Eliezer's opinions were carefully preserved; no one seems to have formulated a legal pericope indicating that Eliezer's laws were not to be taken seriously. We found no evidence, except for Ilai's and Aqiba's lists, of deliberate falsification of Eliezer's opinion to secure acceptance of either what he said or the opposite of what he said. The existence of chains does not lead to the inference that it was necessary to protect particularly controversial opinions by testifying as to their transmission.

Not a single legal tradition is phrased in such a way as to reflect hostility toward Eliezer b. Hyrcanus. Apart from the saying of Ishmael -- contradicted by another -- and the lists of Ilai and Aqiba, we have no evidence that the formulation and transmission of Eliezer's teachings were subject to extraordinary or negative circumstances. Eleazar b. Azariah, Joshua, Gamaliel, and especially Aqiba regularly occur with Eliezer. Whatever the history of those pericopae, it does not include an effort to denigrate Eliezer, whose opinions register at parity with his opposition, whose reasoning is clearly spelled out, and who is treated with unfailing respect. We cannot claim that these are signs of a favorable opinion of Eliezer. But they certainly yield no hint of hostility toward him or his traditions. Overall, the traditions about Eliezer derive from friendly or neutral sources, Aqiban and otherwise. So far as evidence permits, we may suppose those sources include Eliezer's own disciples. Of Ilai there can be no doubt. Aqiba occurs chiefly as an equal; we see no hint that he was Eliezer's disciple. The numerous instances in which Aqiba presents an opinion contrary to Eliezer's do not suggest he was a disciple. But this fact makes all the more striking the considerable involvement of Aqiba in Eliezer's materials.

The earliest Eliezer exhibits no affinity to, or relationship with, Yohanan b. Zakkai, whose name is entirely absent, and whose legal rulings -- such as they may have been at the end of Yavnean times -- are strikingly ignored. Eliezer never appears as a co-disciple with Joshua. If both masters studied with the same authority, we have no evidence of that fact.

Eliezer is not consistently associated with the House of Shammai. In some instances, he rules in a way not inconsistent with the House of Shammai. In others, he seems closer to the Hillelites. In still other pericopae involving the Houses, Eliezer stands apart from the opinions of both. He would seem closer to the Shammaites in six (or five) pericopae, to the Hillelites in five (or six). What is most important is that in none of these cases is association with the House of Shammai regarded as a reason to reject Eliezer's opinion, nor do we see an effort to tie Eliezer to the House of Shammai in order to exclude his opinions from consideration. The picture is confused; I discern no effort at systematization.

The subject-matter of Eliezer's rulings attested at Yavneh covers much the same ground as the Houses' rulings (Phar. III, pp. 223-230), but introduces new issues as well. The two bodies of material compare as follows (""=Eliezer rules on or in the same pericope):

Houses   Eliezer

A. Temple Law, Jerusalem, Pilgrimage, and Priestly Dues

	Houses		Eliezer
1.	Burning unclean with clean meat	1.	""
2.	Laying on of hands	2.	--
3.	Bitter-water ritual	3.	-- (But Eliezer rules on other aspects of the ritual, M. Sot. 1:1.)
4.	Israelites eat first-born with priests	4.	--
5.	Children make pilgrimage	5.	--
6.	--	6.	Cattle given to the Temple are not sacrificed but sold.
7.	--	7.	Liability for lost redemption-lamb set aside for firstling of an ass.
8.	--	8.	One may not dedicate all one's property to Temple.
9-10.	--	9-10.	Preparing Sin-offering water -- two rulings.
11.	--	11.	Whole-offering parts confused with Sin-offering parts are burned together.
12.	--	12.	Blood from blemished offerings mixed with blood from unblemished offerings is sprinkled.
13.	--	13.	Wrong intention renders Meal-offering invalid.

B. Agricultural Tithes, Offerings, and Taboos

	Houses		Eliezer
1.	Unclean Heave-offering mixed with clean (Eliezer b. Hyrcanus)	1.	--
2.	Giving Heave-offering of grapes and the remainder is eventually made into raisins (Eliezer b. Hyrcanus)	2.	--

3. Removing old produce at Nisan   3. --
    (Joshua b. Hananiah)

4. Pe'ah from olives, carobs -- how   4. --
    given (Gamaliel II)

5. Forgotten-sheaf-rules (Eliezer b.   5. --
    'Azariah, Joshua b. Hananiah)

6. Seventh-year-produce rules (Tarfon)   6. --

7. Second-tithe money in Jerusalem   7. --
    (Tarfon, Ben Zoma, Ben 'Azzai,
    Aqiba)

8. Heave-offering vetches (Aqiba)   8. --

9. Fleece-offering (Aqiba)   9. --

10. Date of New Year for trees   10. --
    (Aqiba)

11. Olive-presses in walls of Jerusalem   11. --
    (Aqiba)

12. Fourth-year-fruit rules (Aqiba)   12. --

13. Mixed seeds in vineyard (Aqiba)   13. --

14. Heave-offering from black and   14. ""
    white figs (Ilai)

15. --   15. Clean-Heave-offering for unclean.
                                                       [= No. 2]

16. --   16. Cakes of Thank-offering of Nazirite
                                                       exempt from Dough-offering

17. --   17. 'Orlah-laws abroad

18. -- [But compare No. 10.]   18. Status of etrog

19. --   19. Seventh-Year oil may be used for
                                                       anointing hide.

20. --   20. Dough-offering on 15 Nisan.

21. -- [But compare M. Shev. 4:2B.]   21. First-fruits in garden are guarded,
                                                       therefore liable.

22. --   22. Fruit from abroad is free of liability.

23. --   23. Making olives and grapes into oil and
                                                       wine.

C. Sabbath-Law

1. 'Eruv in public domain (Hananiah,   1. --
    nephew of Joshua)

2. 'Eruv for separate kinds of food   2. --
    (Hananiah, nephew of Joshua)

3.	'Eruv for alley (Eliezer b. Hyrcanus + Aqiba + disciple of Ishmael)	3.	""
4.	Gentile/Sadducee in alley <u>re</u> 'eruv (Gamaliel II = Meir + Judah)	4.	-- [But see No. 7.]
5.	Work started before Sabbath (Aqiba)	5.	--
6.	--	6.	No 'eruv if field has wall.
7.	-- [But see No. 4.]	7.	Failure of partner to participate in 'eruv does not restrict others.
8.	--	8.	Woman may wear tiara on Sabbath.
9.	--	9.	Acquiring a share in the 'eruv.

D. Festival Law

1.	How much does one drink to be liable on the Day of Atonement (Eliezer b. Hyrcanus)	1.	""
2.	Large cakes <u>re</u> Passover (Gamaliel II)	2.	--
3.	Pick pulse on festival (Gamaliel II)	3.	--
4.	Other festival rules (Gamaliel II)	4.	--
5.	Size of <u>Sukkah</u> (Eleazar b. R. Saddoq)	5.	--
6.	--	6.	Hart's-tongue on Passover.
7-10.		7-10.	Rulings on rite of Atonement.
11.	-- [Eliezer attests Houses' dispute, M. Bes. 1:1.]	11.	Egg born on festival.
12.	--	12.	New millstone on festival week.

E. Liturgy

1.	Order of blessing: Oil <u>vs.</u> myrtle (Gamaliel II)	1.	--
2.	Proper position of saying <u>Shema</u> (Eleazar b. 'Azariah, Ishmael, Tarfon)	2.	--
3.	How far recite <u>Hallel</u> at <u>Seder</u> (Tarfon, Aqiba)	3.	--
4.	<u>Tefillin</u> in privy (Aqiba)	4.	--
5.	Where shake <u>Lulav</u> (Aqiba, <u>re</u> Gamaliel, Joshua)	5.	--
6.	Limit <u>re sisit</u> (Jonathan b. Batyra)	6.	--
7.	Circumcision of child born circumcized (Eleazar b. R. Saddoq)	7.	--
8.	--	8.	New Year liturgy (Lev. 23:24).

f. <u>Uncleanness Laws</u>

1.	Quarter-<u>qab</u> of bones in 'Tent' (Joshua b. Hananiah)	1.	--
2.	Woman kneading in 'Tent' (Aqiba, Joshua b. Hananiah)	2.	--
3.	If man shook tree -- preparation for uncleanness by reason of water (Joshua b. Hananiah)	3.	--
4.	Uncleanness of liquids -- Yosi b. Yo'ezer (Eliezer b. Hyrcanus + Aqiba)	4.	""
5.	Uncleanness of scroll-wrappers (Gamaliel II)	5.	--
6.	When do olives receive uncleanness in harvest (Gamaliel II)	6.	--
7.	Mustard-strainer (Eleazar b. R. Saddoq)	7.	--
8.	Itch inside itch (cleanness rite) (Aqiba)	8.	--
9.	Insusceptibility of sheet (Aqiba)	9.	--
10.	Searching grave-area (Aqiba)	10.	--
11.	Issue of semen in third day (Aqiba)	11.	--
12.	Uncleanness of fish (Aqiba)	12.	--
13.	--	13.	Partitions in 'Tent.'
14.	--	14.	Shoe on the last in incomplete, therefore clean.
15.	--	15.	Even though door is open, house is clean -- <u>re</u> 'Tents.'
16.	--	16.	Jars tightly covered with bit of corpse inside.
17.		17.	Dirt from grave-area.
18.	--	18.	Leprosy sign deliberately removed.
19.	--	19.	Ritual status of honey-comb.

G. <u>Civil Law, Torts, and Damages. Criminal Law.</u>

1.	Damaged bailment (Aqiba)	1.	--
2.	--	2.	Woman hanged +/- naked.

H. Family Law and Inheritances

1.	Vow not to have intercourse (Eliezer)	1.	[May not be our Eliezer.]
2.	Husband's inheritance when wife dies as a minor (Eliezer b. Hyrcanus)	2.	""
3.	Signs of adulthood (Eliezer b. Hyrcanus)	3.	""
4.	Levirate rules re brothers married to sisters (Eliezer b. Hyrcanus, Eleazar b. 'Azariah, Abba Saul)	4.	""
5.	Levirate rules re co-wives (Tarfon, Eleazar b. 'Azariah, Aqiba, Joshua b. Hananiah)	5.	--
6.	Test rags for each act of intercourse (Joshua b. Hananiah).	6.	--
7.	Sanctifies property and intends to divorce wife (Joshua b. Hananiah + Eliezer b. Hyrcanus)	7.	""
8.	Wife remarries on testimony of one witness (Aqiba, Gamaliel II).	8.	--
9.	Grounds for divorce (Aqiba)	9.	--
10.	Dividing estate where order of deaths is unclear (Aqiba)	10.	--
11.	Blood of woman who has given birth and not immersed (Eliezer).	11.	""
12.	-- [But see No. 2.]	12.	Deed of a female-minor is null.
13.	--	13.	Levir refused by minor.
14.	-- [But see No. 9.]	14.	Conditional divorce valid.
15.	--	15.	Minor who has exercised right of refusal still controls usufruct of melog. [= 12]

I. Miscellany

1.	Taboo against drinking gentile wine (Gamaliel II)	1.	--
2.	Eliezer b. Hyrcanus re overturning couch before festival, b. M.Q. 20a, is given by Eleazar b. R. Simeon as Houses-dispute, Tos. M.Q. 2:9.	2.	""

Eliezer Alone

1. Releasing vows made easy.

2. Gambler may not testify.

3. Samaritan bread permitted to Israelites.

4.   Repent before death.

5.   Many sinful acts of a single type are punished by an equivalent number of Sin-of-
      ferings.

6.   Spinning blue-wool for fringe.

7-9. Nazir who contracts uncleanness on last day of his period -- various rulings.

The themes of Eliezer's rulings are much the same as those of the Houses, and the
proportions seem about right, with one exception. In this stratum Eliezer is strikingly
silent on liturgical matters. This would accord with the (presently unattested) ruling that
a fixed liturgy is not to be followed; if so, Eliezer would not issue many rulings on the
subject.

       But the substance in detail of Eliezer's rulings strikingly differs from that of the
Houses. Eliezer paid attention to dedications to the Temple; the pericopae of the Houses
attested at Yavneh ignore the subject. He has important rulings on the preparation of
Sin-offering water -- and others, not attested at Yavneh, are likely to be valid traditions.
The Houses do not rule on the subject. He solves through logic various problems of
mixtures of diverse holy materials and how they are to be disposed of. The Houses do not
enter that problem at all. He deals -- at length, as we shall see later on -- with the
problem of intention in the cult. The Houses do not. His rulings on the Temple thus
concern strikingly fundamental matters. The tendency of those rulings is to figure out the
logic and consistent order to be imposed on the Temple cult. What actually was done
never enters his framework of discussion. He seems to have attempted to develop a
coherent and internally logical set of rules on the Temple cult and its conduct.

       While some of the rules on agricultural taboos concern both the Houses and Eliezer,
others involve Eliezer alone. These tend to represent striking innovations in antecedent
laws. Two themes seem important, first, the status of the produce of foreign countries;
second, and of fundamental importance, the easing of the distinctions in produce subject
to Heave-offering.

       As to Sabbath law, for both the Houses and Eliezer the 'eruv appears as a pre-
dominate concern. In respect to festival law, Eliezer has important new rulings on the
rite of the Day of Atonement -- appropriate for his agendum for the Temple, which
concentrates on the conduct of the cult.

       The subject-matter of the uncleanness rules is pretty much the same, but the
specific rulings of Eliezer are original. Again, we observe a tendency to solve a problem
through abstract reasoning, rather than through a simple edict or citation of established
practice. This would account for the difference between the discrete rules attributed to
the Houses on when and whether various objects are susceptible to uncleanness, in
contrast to Eliezer's effort on the same themes to give reasons for rulings, applying to
more than the single case at hand.

       Civil and criminal law is virtually ignored by both the Houses and Eliezer.

The interest in family law and inheritances is much the same; vows, inheritances, Levirate rules, and divorce concern both parties. But Eliezer's generalization about the nullity of the deed of a female minor and the rule, susceptible to generalization and expansion, about the conditional divorce, are unknown to the Houses and constitute far-reaching theoretical innovations.

Entirely new legal themes involve releasing vows, rules of testimony, the law of the Nazirite who has become unclean, and the general principle about liability for various similar sinful acts. These do not yield complete new agenda of legislative legal interest. But they are, individually, quite novel topics, on which the Yavnean pericopae of the Houses are silent. The Mishnaic evidence deals, therefore, with the following:

Temple and Priesthood: Nos. 1, 7, 14

Agricultural Rules: Nos. 4, 17

Festival Law: Nos. 5, 6

Liturgy: Nos. 3, 8, 9, 10

Uncleanness Laws: Nos. 2, 15, 18

Civil Law, Torts, Damages, Criminal Law: Nos. 11, 12, 13

Family Law and Inheritances: --

Pre-70 Pharisees and Eliezer tend to rule primarily on agricultural law, Sabbath and festival rules, and uncleanness. Yohanan's traditions are scattered; most of those on the festival have to do with the problems posed by the Destruction. The law in Nos. 11, 12, 17 and 18 is not accredited to Yohanan; he simply approves what others have done. In all, Yohanan's legal agenda hardly correspond to those of the pre-70 Houses -- about which he knows nothing -- and seem on the whole to focus upon the Temple, the priests, and the liturgical consequence of the Destruction, rather than upon any other matter. The greater number of his other rulings has to do with Sabbath and festival laws. To be sure, the whole thing adds up to very little. But while, on the basis of the extant laws, one may reasonably claim Eliezer was a Pharisee, on the same basis one cannot claim the same for Yohanan. At best one may say he _might_ have been a Pharisee. The external evidence does not help; Luke-Acts knows Gamaliel; Josephus know Simeon b. Gamaliel; but no external source knows about Yohanan, despite the decisive role in events of the day claimed for him by the later story-tellers.

The earliest Eliezer therefore stands within the framework of pre-70 Pharisaism. We need not doubt he was one of the major continuators of the sect. Assuming he came to Yavneh as an adult, he probably had sound information on the sect's beliefs and practices before 70. This makes all the more interesting the striking innovations he evidently introduced. The chief one would seem to be the tendency to work out the logic behind discrete rulings or to apply logic to superficially unrelated problems. A second would be the extension of the legal agenda to include the exact conduct of the Temple cult. Whether or not others were preserving a record of what had been done in Jerusalem, Eliezer certainly attempted to produce an orderly account of what should be done in the future. But his rulings pertain to exceptional and theoretical circumstances -- mixtures of holy materials which should not normally be mixed up -- and this must mean that the basic procedures of the Temple were well-established and acceptable to him. A third innovation is the effort to simplify what may formerly have been complicated and perhaps internally contradictory rules, for example, on the status of the female-minor, the releasing of vows, the giving of Heave-offering from related, but slightly different substances, and the like. In all these matters Eliezer seems to have sought to impose a single, comprehensive, and on the whole, lenient rule, one which in general would uncomplicate the status of individuals and straighten out the complex application of taboos. In all, therefore, the earliest Eliezer emerges as an important, original lawyer. His legal rulings were carefully worked out and transmitted in the circle of the leading authority of the following generation, Aqiba, and involved the major figures of his own day, particularly Aqiba, Joshua, Gamaliel, and Eleazar b. ^CAzariah.

CHAPTER FOUR
THE BETTER AND THE FAIR TRADITIONS

i. The Aqiban Eliezer

It is generally taken for granted that the founders of the Ushan academy consisted of the disciples of Aqiba, so that Ushan traditions are based primarily upon, or evolve from, the Aqiban part of the Yavnean corpus. Whether this supposition is correct or not I cannot say. But it is certainly a fact that the largest number of pericopae attested at Yavneh for which we are at all able to propose a redactional authority are to be attributed to Ilai, and he was Eliezer's disciple. By contrast, what bears Ushan names is attested by people supposedly disciples of Aqiba. It follows that the better traditions represent a distinct strand in the whole corpus of Eliezer's materials. They bear not only a later attestation, but also a quite different probable point of origin, with Aqiba's disciples at Usha. If Aqiba studied with Eliezer, they should be not much less reliable than the best traditions, attested by Ilai, except that they stand one step removed from Eliezer, with the disciple's disciples, rather than the disciple himself, taking the chief part in their formulation and redaction. This trait becomes evident in the Ushans' difficulty in agreeing upon the definition of the protases of Eliezer's pericopae. They had in common a thematic agenda, but not much else.

ii. Examples of the Laws

Neutralizing Heave-Offering

Tos. Ter. 5:10-11/M. Ter. 4:8-11 deal with neutralizing Heave-offering which has fallen into a large quantity of secular produce. Eliezer holds a hundred and one parts are required to neutralize; Joshua, a hundred and a bit more -- a negligible difference.

Joshua then holds (M. Ter. 4:8) that black figs neutralize white, and vice versa; Eliezer denies it. Aqiba says if one knows what has fallen into the mixture, the black cannot neutralize the white, but if not, they can -- essentially Eliezer's opinion.

In Tos. Ter. 5:10, Meir and Judah differ on the opinions of Eliezer and Joshua. Meir holds Eliezer's opinion is that when what has fallen in is known, it will not neutralize, but when not, it will; Joshua says whether known or unknown, it will not neutralize. So Meir's Eliezer is the same as the Mishnah's, but his Joshua is in a position still more strict than the Mishnah's Eliezer.

Judah then says Eliezer says, Whether known or not known, it will not neutralize; and Joshua says, Whether known or not known, it will neutralize; Judah introduces Aqiba's compromise. Thus Meir's Eliezer is Judah's Aqiba; Meir's Joshua is Judah's Eliezer! Meir clearly has placed Eliezer in the position of his teacher, Aqiba -- about whose involvement in the pericope Meir knows nothing. Similarly in Tos. Ter. 5:11 Judah has Eliezer in the strict position, but then defines for Joshua a still more strict opinion.

What is attested by the Ushans, therefore, is that the early Yavneans disputed about the principles of the neutralization of Heave-offering. But exactly what position was held by which master cannot be said to have been clearly known at Usha, if, as is obvious, a wide range of positions leaves room for several, incompatible opinions to be assigned to each master. While from the best traditions we derive knowledge of the exact opinions held by Eliezer, from the better ones we'seem reliably to locate the themes or legal agenda on which he evidently laid down laws, but not the exact opinions he actually held.

Nor can we extrapolate from the best to the better traditions an opinion which Eliezer ought, on the basis of the former, to have held in connection with the latter. We have no clear idea of Eliezer's tendency in the materials before us. To be sure, he ruled in a lenient way about giving Heave-offering from clean to unclean produce. But that does not justify supposing that here, too, he would rule, in a lenient spirit, that the Heave-offering may be easily neutralized, for the legal principles are not the same and are not even related.

Circumcision and the Sabbath

Tos. Shab. 15:10/M. Shab. 19:4 deals with circumcision on the Sabbath. The attested issue concerns a child supposed to be circumcized after the Sabbath, who is actually circumcized on the Sabbath. Eliezer and Joshua, according to Simeon b. Yohai, agree that the man is liable. But if the child is to be circumcized on Friday, and the operation is done on the Sabbath, Eliezer declares the man liable for Sin-offering. Then a debate is supplied.

M. Shab. 19:4 has a confusion of two babies, but the problem is the same: circumcizing on the Sabbath when it is not the eighth day after birth. Then, in b. Shab. 137a, Simeon b. Eleazar has them disagree on a confusion of two infants; Meir attests a dispute on the same case, but on different days. Simeon b. Eleazar deals with Friday and Saturday; Meir, Saturday and Sunday. These constitute strong attestations not only for the theme of the dispute, but also of Eliezer's opinion in principle. Eliezer certainly holds that one who circumcizes on the Sabbath when that is not the eighth day after birth will be liable to a Sin-offering. According to M. Shab. 19:4, the obligation to circumcize is such that if the eighth day does not coincide with the Sabbath, the obligation is sufficiently diminished so that one should not do so on the Sabbath.

M. Shab. 19:1 has Eliezer take a lenient position with respect to Aqiba's. One may do anything at all in respect to a circumcision on the Sabbath. Aqiba holds one may do on the Sabbath only what cannot be done beforehand, that is, the actual operation. Judah the Patriarch attests to this dispute, but the construction of Tos. Shab. 15:16, involving Yosi b. Halafta, then Eliezer and Aqiba, is such that 19:1 ought to be accorded an Ushan attestation as well.

If so, we have two opinions for Eliezer, one quite lenient, allowing anything at all to be done in connection with a circumcision on the Sabbath, the other quite strict, holding that an error in circumcizing on the Sabbath a child that needs to be circumcized on some other day produces the liability to a Sin-offering. These principles are not in contradiction. The leniency of the first imposes the strictness of the second: one may do what needs to be done on the Sabbath, but one must be sure that the operation actually has to be performed on the Sabbath. The pericope is not hostile.

iii. Eliezer at Usha: The Houses

The better traditions know nothing about Eliezer as a Shammaite. The only pertinent pericope has him as a Hillelite. The issue of Eliezer's relations to the Houses is scarcely raised.

The comparison of Eliezer's Ushan attestations and those of the Houses is clear in the following (Phar. III, pp. 231-233):

Houses   Eliezer

A. History

	Houses		Eliezer
1.	Echo to Simeon the Just and Yohanan the High Priest (Judah b. Baba)	1.	--
2.	Echo to Hillel, Samuel the Small, etc. (Judah b. Baba)	2.	-- [Eliezer added much later]
3.	Hillel came up at 40 (Post-Aqibans?)	3.	--
4.	Rise of Hillel (Tos. Pisha 4:13)	4.	--
5.	Hillel expounded language of common folk (Meir + Judah?)	5.	--
6.	Disputes come from poor (Yosi)	6.	--
7.	End of Grapeclusters (Judah b. Baba)	7.	--
8.	Trough of Jehu (Judah b. Ilai)	8.	--
9.	Hillel: Scatter/gather (Simeon b. Yohai)	9.	--
10.	Who prepared heifer-sacrifices (Meir)	10.	--
11.	Lay/not lay (Meir + Judah)	11.	--
12.	Temple of Onias (Meir + Judah)	12.	--
13.	Simeon b. Shetah vs. Judah b. Tabbai as Nasi (Meir + Judah)	13.	--
14.	Letter of Gamaliel to Diaspora (Judah)	14.	--
15.	Yohanan b. Gudgada's sons (Judah)	15.	--

B. Temple Law, Jerusalem, Pilgrimage, and Priestly Dues

	Houses		Eliezer
1.	Two sprinklings of sacrificial blood (Eliezer b. Jacob)	1.	--
2.	Coins for sheqel (Simeon b. Yohai)	2.	--
3.	Burn Flesh inside/outside (Meir + Judah)	3.	--
4.	--	4.	The Passover slaughtered for some other purpose (M. Pes. 6:5/Tos. Pis. 5:4 + M. Zev. 1:1 etc.) (Simeon b. Yohai)
5.	--	5.	Impairment in sacrificial process (Tos. Zev. 4:1, M. Me. 1:2-3, etc.) (Simeon, Yosi)
6.	--	6.	Progeny of Peace-offerings (M. Tem. 3:1) (Simeon)

| 7. | -- | 7. | Sin-offering when in doubt (M. Ker. 4:2-3/Tos. Ker. 2:12-15, etc.) (Yosi, Simeon Shezuri, Simeon b. Yohai) |

C. Agricultural Tithes, Offerings, and Taboos

1.	Watering plants until New Year of Seventh Year (Yosi b. Kifar, or Eleazar b. R. Saddoq)	1.	--
2.	Israelite woman eats Terumah (Yosi)	2.	--
3.	Dough for Hallah (Yosi)	3.	--
4.	Heave-offering of oil for crushed olives (Yosi)	4.	--
5.	Produce not fully harvested passed through Jerusalem (Yosi)	5.	--
6.	Olive-presses in walls of Jerusalem (Yosi)	6.	--
7.	Demai re comer (Simeon b. Yohai)	7.	--
8.	Demai re Hallah (Simeon b. Yohai)	8.	--
9.	Change silver and produce (Meir)	9.	--
10.	Heave-offering of fenugreek (Meir + Judah)	10.	--
11.	Fruit of prepared field in Seventh Year (Judah)	11.	--
12.	Vineyard patch (Judah)	12.	--
13.	Burn doubtful Heave-offering (Judah)	13.	--
14.	Young shoot over stone (Simeon b. Gamaliel, Yosi + Meir)	14.	--
15.	Assigning produce to past/coming year re pod (Simeon b. Gamaliel)	15.	--
16.	Fruit of fourth year vineyard re Fifth, Removal (Simeon b. Gamaliel)	16.	--
17.	Demai re sweet oil (Nathan)	17.	--
18.	--	18.	Forgotten sheaves (Houses) (Tos. Pe'ah 3:2)
19.	--	19.	Handkerchiefs and 'Diverse kinds' (Tos. Kil. 5:18) (Meir + Judah)
20.	--	20.	Neutralizing Heave-offering (Tos. Ter. 5:10-11) (Meir + Judah)
21.	--	21.	Definition of liquids (M. Ter. 11:2, Tos. Ter. 9:9) (Nathan, Meir, Jacob, Judah, Rabbi)
22.	--	22.	Burning clean and unclean Heave-offering -- Hames together (M. Pes. 1:7, Tos. Pis. 1:5) (Yosi)
23.	--	23.	Saffron not purchased with Tithe-money (Tos. M.S. 1:14) (Simeon)

D. Sabbath Law

1.	Clearing table on Sabbath (Yosi)	1.	--
2.	Work started before Sabbath, completed on Sabbath (Yosi)	2.	--
3.	cEruv with Sadducee (Meir + Judah)	3.	--
4.	Put back on stove (Meir + Judah)	4.	--
5.	Food for Sabbath (Judah)	5.	--

6.	Work to gentile launderer before Sabbath (Simeon b. Gamaliel)	6. --
7.	Charity on Sabbath (Simeon b. Gamaliel)	7. --
8.	CEruv for cistern (Simeon b. Gamaliel)	8. --
9.	--	9. Completing the eating of a grapecluster (Tos. Ter. 7:10C) (Nathan) N.B. Compare the Houses in Nos. 2 and 5 above.
10.	--	10. Circumcision and Sabbath (Tos. Shab. 15:10/M. Shab. 19:4) (Yosi, Simeon b. Eleazar, Simeon b. Yohai)
[11.	--	11. Making two Ceruvs (Tos. Eruv. 4:1-2) (Judah b. Ilai)]
12.	--	12. Acquiring an Ceruv (M. Eruv. 7:11) (Judah b. Ilai)

E. Festival Law

1.	Proselyte on day before Passover (Yosi)	1. --
2.	Gifts on festival (Yosi + Judah)	2. --
3.	Return pesah whole (Simeon b. Yohai)	3. --
4.	Tying pigeon (Simeon b. Yohai)	4. Below, No. 12.
5.	Egg laid on festival (Meir)	5. As above.
6.	Prepare spices, salt on festival (Meir)	6. --
7.	Timber-roofing of Sukkah (Meir + Judah)	7. --
8.	Pick pulse on festival (Judah)	8. --
9.	More vessels on account of need (Simeon b. Gamaliel)	9. --
10.	--	10. Measure of dough for Passover (Tos. Pis. 3:8) (Nathan)
11.	--	11. Cone-shaped Sukkah (b. Suk. 19b/M. Suk. 1:11) (Nathan)
12.	Above, No. 4.	12. May use splinter (Tos. Y.T. 3:18M. Bes. 4:6-7) (Simeon b. Yohai)

F. Liturgy

1.	Order of Havdalah (Meir + Judah)	1. --
2.	--	2. Powers of rain (M. Ta. 1:1) (Judah)

G. Uncleanness Laws

1.	Vessels before Cam ha'ares (Dosetai b. R. Yannai)	1. --
2.	Uncleanness of weasel (Yosi)	2. --
3.	Burn clean and unclean meat together (Yosi)	3. --
4.	Measure chest (Yosi)	4. --
5.	Split in roof (Yosi)	5. --
6.	Gather grapes in grave-area (Yosi)	6. --
7.	Lid-chain connector (Yosi)	7. --
8.	Place water (M. Maksh. 1:4) (Yosi + Judah)	8. --
9.	Vessel under waterspout (Yosi +	9. --

10.	Water from roof leaked into jar (Yosi + Meir)	10.	--
11.	Uncleanness of <u>Qohelet</u> (Yosi + Simeon)	11.	--
12.	Uncleanness of girdle (Simeon b. Simeon)	12.	--
13.	Removing pot for Heave-offering (Simeon b. Yohai)	13.	--
14.	Uncleanness of her who has difficulty giving birth (Simeon b. Yohai)	14.	--
15.	Sin-offering water that has fulfilled its purpose (Simeon b. Yohai)	15.	--
16.	How much lacking in skull (Tent) (Meir)	16.	--
17.	When is tube clean (Meir + Judah)	17.	--
18.	When is sheet clean (Meir + Judah)	18.	--
19.	Stool on baking-trough (Meir + Judah)	19.	--
20.	Menstrual blood of gentile woman (Meir + Judah)	20.	--
21.	Quarter-<u>qab</u> of bones in tent (Judah)	21.	--
22.	When to make the vat unclean (Judah)	22.	--
23.	Open hole to let out uncleanness (Judah)	23.	--
24.	Anoint self with clean oil (Judah)	24.	--
25.	Blood of carcass (Judah)	25.	--
26.	Water-skin (Judah)	26.	--
27.	Sell food to <u>haver</u> (Simeon b. Gamaliel)	27.	--
28.	When it ritual pool deemed clean (Simeon b. Gamaliel)	28.	--
29.	--	29.	Cleaning a metal vessel (Tos. Kel. B.M. 4:14/M. Kel. 14:7) (Nathan)
30.	--	30.	Money-pouch (M. Kel. 26:2/Tos. Kel. B.B. 4:3) (Nathan)
31.	--	31.	Jars containing remnant of corpse (Tos. Ah. 9:7) (Judah)
32.	--	32.	Corpse:piece on threshhold (Tos. Ah. 13:10/M. Oh. 17:8) (Simeon b. Yohai)
33.	--	33.	Intention in Sin-offering water (M. Par. 9:4/Tos. Par. 9:6) (Yosi)
34.	--	34.	Moisture of crushed olives (M. Toh. 9:3) (Simeon b. Yohai)
35.	--	35.	<u>Zab</u> (Tos. Nid. 9:13/M. Nid. 10:3) (Yosi, Simeon)
36.	--	36.	Olive's bulk of flesh from living person unclean (M. Ed. 6:2-3/Tos. Ah. 2:7) (Simeon)
37.	--	37.	Connector in bed (Tos. Kel. B.M. 8:8/M. Kel. 18:9) (Simeon b. Yohai)

H. Civil Law, Torts, and Damages

1.	Hillel and futures (usury) (Meir, Judah, Simeon)	1.	--

2. Restore beam or value (Simeon b.   2.   --
    Gamaliel

I. Family Law and Inheritances

1.	Lewdness with minor son (Yosi)	1. --
2.	Cohabitation with mother-in-law (Yosi + Judah)	2. --
3.	Girl married before flow (Meir, Simeon b. Gamaliel, Judah)	3. --
4.	Nursing mother remarries (Meir + Judah)	4. --
5.	Betrothed woman disposes of goods (Judah)	5. --
6.	How many children before desisting from marital life (Nathan)	6. --
7.	Annuling daughter's vows (Nathan)	7. --
8.	Three betrothed woman -- witness/ agent (Nathan)	8. --
9.	--	9. Halisah with wooden sandal (Tos. Yev. 12:11) (Judah)
10.	--	10. Ransoming a wife (Nathan)
11.	--	11. Attesting a writ of divorce (M. Git. 1:1-2) (Judah)
12.	--	12. Dedicating property and paying the Ketuvah (M. Ar. 6:1) (Simeon b. Gamaliel)
13.	--	13. Warning wife before witnesses (M. Sot. 1:1/Tos. Sot. 1:1) (Yosi b. R. Judah)

J. Miscellany

1.	Targum of Job (Yosi)	1. --
2.	Nazir: Erroneous vow (Yosi; Judah)	2. --
3.	Chicken and cheese (Yosi)	3. --
4.	Nazirite vow for longer period (Judah)	4. --
5.	--	5. Repeating a lesson (b. Eruv. 54b) Judah b. Ilai)
6.	--	6. Generation of wilderness in world to come (Tos. Sanh. 13:2) (Joshua b. Qorha)
7.	--	7. Slaughter (Tos. Hul. 2:11) (Simeon b. Yohai)

The Ushan attestations of Eliezer's traditions differ from those of the Houses' materials in two important respects. First, the Ushans have no traditions in Eliezer's name on any historical question pertaining to either pre- or post-70 times. Second, Eliezer's Temple laws attested by Ushans greatly exceed in numbers and importance the Houses' equivalent materials -- a pattern already observed in the best traditions. I see no Ushan expansion in the range of interests attributed to Eliezer. In general, as in the Yavnean materials, so in the Ushan ones, with the noted exception, Eliezer rules on pretty much the same legal agenda as were faced by the Houses and in roughly the same proportions.

But the subject-matter of Eliezer's rulings bears slight relationship to that of those of the Houses attested at Usha. We find no points of contact. Apart from the considerable, but familiar, innovation in his theorizing on the cult, we find a wide range of unrelated rulings, none with a parallel among the Houses'. The only set bearing a general resemblance to Houses' rulings pertains to issues of ritual uncleanness.

iv. Eliezer in the Better Traditions

The better traditions exhibit no importance differences from the best ones. The Ushan Eliezer stands within the framework both of pre-70 Pharisaism and of the Yavnean Eliezer. The Ushans seem to have innovated little, if at all, in the themes of laws attributed to Eliezer. The Ushan attestations serve to establish the agenda on which Eliezer legislated, but provide little evidence of the exact opinions which he held or were attributed to him.

Let us review the main results of a survey of the better traditions. Eliezer ruled on whether the taboo against 'Diverse Kinds' applies to handkerchiefs, scroll-wrappers, and bath towels. He legislated on mixtures of one hundred-and-one parts of secular produce and one part of Heave-offering, in general taking a more lenient position than Joshua. He said, again in the lenient position, that a deed begun licitly might be completed even illicitly. He and Joshua debated the definition of liquids capable of rendering produce susceptible to uncleanness. In respect to circumcision on the Sabbath, he held that performing such an act when it is not actually required -- that is, not on the eighth day -- will produce liability to a Sin-offering. He ruled one may acquire an 'eruv with coins. He taught a law with respect to memorizing traditions: the master must teach a tradition four times. He said one might not burn unclean Heave-offering-hames with clean. He stated that a Passover-sacrifice offered for some other purpose than the Passover will impose liability for a Sin-offering -- this on the basis of logic. A cone-shaped Sukkah is not acceptable; the Sukkah must have a roof. Like the House of Hillel, he taught that one might use on the festival what was not set aside on the preceding day. The Powers of Rain-prayer is to be said from the first, not the last, day of Sukkot. One who has forbidden his wife from benefitting from him must nonetheless redeem her if she is taken captive, as explicitly required by the Ketuvah. He glossed a rule about bringing a writ of divorce from foreign parts, applying the rule even to neighboring villages. He held that sprinkling the blood when the meat-offering is impaired is of no effect; conversely, if the sprinkling of the blood has not properly taken place, the meat-offering is likewise unacceptable. The progeny of Peace-offerings may not be brought as Peace-offerings. An important general rule is that when one is not certain exactly what sin he has done or even whether he has sinned at all, he must still bring a Sin-offering. A metal-vessel in parts may contract uncleanness and be cleansed. A money-bag or a pearl-pouch is capable of receiving uncleanness. He gave several rules in respect to 'Tents.' Sin-offering-water may be rendered unfit by the wrong intention, even though one has not actually done anything to carry out his intention. He ruled on the moisture exuded by crushed olives or by the olive vat. He decreed in a lenient way concerning the ritual cleanness of a Zab who examined himself only on the first and seventh day of his period of uncleanness. He held that an olive's bulk of flesh from the limb of a living person is capable of conveying uncleanness. And he held that the generation of the Wilderness would acquire a portion in the world to come.

As stated, the themes are already familiar from the best traditions: agricultural laws, a few Sabbath and festival rules, some teachings on the matter of marriage and divorce, and ritual uncleanness. The cult, in theory if not in practice, continued to take an important place in his traditions, and the method of producing laws on the cult -- logic rather than tradition -- continued as before. No area of law dealt with in the best traditions is neglected in the better ones; no legal theme is introduced to the already established agendum. The specific opinions, to be sure, are on different subjects. But we are unable to find contradictions between principles used in deciding cases in the best traditions and those employed in the better ones. We observe an essential consistency between Yavnean and Ushan materials, both in an affirmative sense, in the selection of legal problems, and in a negative sense, in the absence of contradictions of established principles. This seems to me a considerable argument in favor of the authenticity of the laws attributed to Eliezer.

In all of these traditions we discern not the slightest hint of hostility toward Eliezer. Detailed rules of course occur here which have not been seen before. But if the Ushan Eliezer is the Aqiban Eliezer, then we may say that no important trait of Ilai's Eliezer is absent in Aqiba's; both schools or circles seem to have a fairly consistent and harmonious picture of the man. The two sets of traditions differ only in the degree of accuracy imputed to the one over the other. Among the best traditions we seem to find reliable evidence about specific opinions; among the better ones, usable data are chiefly about probable themes, but not commonly about the exact legal opinion to be attributed to Eliezer. Where we have some evidence on the formation of Eliezer's traditions and how the responsible tradent knew what he attributed to Eliezer, we thus find a single picture of the man. And that picture emerges from a wide range of authorities, who cannot be thought to have conspired with one another to make up a false view or to have laid down laws in Eliezer's name on the basis of a plan to misrepresent him.

v. The Authenticity of Pericopae First Appearing in Mishnah-Tosefta

Of the approximately 130 pericopae which occur with attestation only of appearance in Mishnah-Tosefta (catalogued in Eliezer II, pp. 170-200), the following clearly represent extensions or applications of principles already attested in the Yavnean and Ushan strata or have some other sort of earlier attestation:

Nos. 5-6: Judah rules in harmony with Eliezer; No. 7: Thorns in the vineyard; No. 8: Judah accords with Eliezer; No. 9; No. 11; No. 13: Mixture of prohibited and permitted substances; No. 14: Give better for worse Heave-offering; No. 15: Taking action to prevent a transgression; No. 16: Liquid renders susceptible; Nos. 17-19: Intention; No. 20; No. 21: Intention; No. 22: Rabbi and Yosah attest; No. 23: Judah; No. 25: Simeon, Judah, Rabbi attest the law, but not Eliezer's particular opinion; No. 26B: 'Orlah -- what is prohibited remains separate; No. 27: Licit action may be completed; No. 29: Intention; No. 30; No. 34: Circumcision on Sabbath (Usha + Rabbi); No. 35 = No. 34 (?); No. 37; No. 38 = No. 34 (pre-Usha?); No. 39: Yosi attests re distant journey; No. 43: Judah may attest; No. 43; No. 44 (may be Yavnean); Nos. 45-46: Judah may attest; No. 50: Sin-offering for each sin of a single type; Nos. 55-56: Releasing vows made easy; No. 57: Same principle as No. 56; No. 58. Sprinkling required for meat -- Joshua may attest principle of Eliezer's ruling; No. 61; Woman regarded negatively; No. 62; No. 66D: Apportioning goods verbally -- Meir, Judah attest; No. 67; No. 68; No. 69: Simeon attests; No. 72; No. 73; No. 75 = No. 67; No. 77; No. 78; No. 82; No. 92 -- Simeon; Nos. 100-104, 106-110: Red Heifer-rules show Eliezer's established tendency to rule leniently in this matter, and Judah rules consistently with Eliezer.

The following deal with legal topics already familiar in earlier strata:

Nos. 5-6: Liability for Pe'ah and defective clusters; No. 10: Seventh Year; No. 12: Heave-offering; No. 24: Liability for Dough-offering; No. 26A: 'Orlah; No. 28: Sabbath-carrying; No. 31: Sabbath-scratching; No. 32: Sabbath-weaving; No. 33: Sabbath-building; No. 40: Atonement-rite; No. 41: Building on festival; No. 47: Female minor re divorce; No. 48: Levir-marriage; No. 49: Remarriage on testimony of one witness; Nos. 51-54: Virginity claims; No. 59: Nazir; No. 60: Nazir (may be Yavnean); No. 71: redeem firstling; No. 76: Progeny of terefah; Nos. 83, 84, 85, 86, 87, 88, 89, 90, 91, 93, 94, 95, 96, 97: Uncleanness; Nos. 98, 99: Leprosy signs; No. 105: Red Heifer rite; Nos. 111, 111A: Uncleanness; No. 112: Ritual pool; Nos. 113-115: Ritual pool; Nos. 116-117: Uncleanness of Zabah; Nos. 118-120; Zab; No. 126: Tithes from Ammon and Moab.

The following treat new subjects, heretofore not part of Eliezer's traditions:

Nos. 1-4: The Shema' and the Prayer; No. 36; On that day; Nos. 63-65: Neglected corpse; No. 66: Mamzer (?); No. 66A: Fire-damage; No. 66B: Dogs; No. 66C: Acquire property through walking (?); No. 66E: Trial of animals; No. 70: Cock-partridge (?); No. 74: Oxen as pledge (?); No. 121: After Temple was destroyed; No. 122: Wise sayings; No. 123: Temple walls; No. 124: Sorcery; No. 125: Minut; No. 128: Gentiles in the world to come.

We therefore observe an astonishing continuity between the legal agenda and even of legal principles attested before Mishnah-Tosefta and those first represented in the final compilations. Of 130 items, only 21 are on entirely new legal or other problems -- approximately 16.1%. Of these, Nos. 36, 121, 122, 123, 125, and 128 are not on legal subjects at all. This leaves fifteen items for the theme of which we might have antici-pated some sort of antecedent evidence. But of these fifteen, Nos. 66, 66C, 66E, 70, and 74 cannot be shown certainly to belong to our Eliezer; the warrant for each is unsubstan-tial. That leaves ten, or approximately 7.6% -- a negligible portion of the total. Of these, the four traditions on the Shema' and the Prayer are part of a much larger set of Yavnean materials on that and related liturgical subjects. The problem is by no means alien to the circle of early Yavnean masters. We have no good reason based on theme alone to suppose Eliezer would not have issued rulings on such matters. As to the three on the neglected corpse (Nos. 63-65), the estimate on fire-damage, the rule against raising dogs, and the trial of animals, matters are not so clear.

The dominant tendency of the stratum marked by first appearance in Mish-nah-Tosefta, strikingly, is not to invent for Eliezer rulings on issues not earlier considered in his legal traditions or principles formerly unrepresented in his laws. Just as we noticed (Phar. III, pp. 209ff.) that the Ushans did not appreciably expand the legal agenda on which rulings were issued in the names of the Houses, so with Eliezer we see that the earliest legal agenda in general remain normative later on. New specific problems will be worked out, to be sure, but if Eliezer in the Yavnean and Ushan strata has nothing to say on an important legal theme, the chances are excellent that nothing on said theme will be attributed to him in Mishnah-Tosefta.

The abundant evidence that a large proportion of materials first given in Mish-nah-Tosefta represents nothing more than the extension of Eliezer's principles to new details supports this contention. Of the approximately 130 pericopae, we found no fewer than 60 attested by earlier masters either in detail or in the operative principle -- 46.1%. The stability of the legal agenda is still further indicated by the final group; 51 pericopae, or 39.2%, deal with already well-attested legal themes, though the specific problems and the same principles are not necessarily attested in the earlier strata. So approximately 86.1% of pericopae whose themes or detailed laws first occur in Mishnah-Tosefta represent nothing more than the continuation of either the identical principles or the general concerns attributed to Eliezer in earlier strata.

What of the non-legal materials? Nos. 36, 121-123 (124), 125, and 128 are to be regarded as part of a tradition no less authentic than the other items. No. 36 has Eliezer and Joshua discuss on-that-day stories. The issue is simply, What went wrong? That they knew something of the pre-70 history of Pharisaism is hardly incredible. No. 121 is something a master after 70 might have said. The sentiment is perfectly commonplace. We are not certain, to be sure, that in the second century Eliezer b. Hyrcanus was called "the Great." The "three" sayings of M. Avot 2:10 are to be considered only in the context of the structure, attestations, and sources of M. Avot 2. They furthermore form part of the larger problem of Eliezer's relationship to Yohanan b. Zakkai, attested for the first time in M. Yad. 4:3, on the one side, and in M. Avot, on the other. The stories spun out of the repentence-saying make clear that it is our Eliezer who is under discussion. But for M. Avot, no one can doubt it. I am unable to interpret the balanced sayings about the Temple in M. Ed. They would seem to be of legal importance. Joshua's, in the same place, asserts that it is permissible to sacrifice even without the Temple, an astonishing saying. But I do not see how Eliezer's is related.

The important items are Nos. 124 and 125. Both are complex, in the one case because of the attribution of the same saying to several masters; in the other, because of the complicated development of materials finally put together in Tos. But both seem of considerable historical interest.

No. 126 makes much of Eliezer's connection to Yohanan; but Eliezer contributes no independent tradition. Eliezer's saying that the gentiles have no portion in the world to come accords with the xenophobia characteristic of post-70 and post-135 times.

Excluding the "three" sayings and the connection to Yohanan, we may then observe that the sum of the biographical materials on Eliezer in the strata ending with Mish-nah-Tosefta consists of a story connecting Eliezer to minim, on the one side, and to sorcery, on the other -- and these are a commonplace combination, with rabbinic stories about Jesus as a sorcerer well attested by the time of Justin (Phar. I, p. 86).

Eliezer's relationships to the Houses figure directly or indirectly in the following:

1. Eliezer agrees with, or rules according to the principles attributed to, the House of Shammai: No. 7: Intention; No. 11: By favor/not by favor; No. 21: Intention; No. 34: In b. Shab. 130b -- Rabbi says Eliezer is a Shammaite, but y. 19:1 says Rabbi ruled according to Eliezer; No. 26: Declaration of betrothal acquires woman; No. 59: Perpetual sanctity takes precedence.

2. Eliezer agrees with, or rules according to the principles attributed to, the House of Hillel: No. 27; No. 36: On that day; No. 38: Eliezer argues as does Hillel; No. 47: Divorced orphan.

Eliezer is thus represented as a Shammaite or rules according to Shammaite principles but is not explicitly so represented in six pericopae; he appears to be a Hillelite in four. The matter can hardly be said to have been settled in the Mishnah-Toseftan stratum. Indeed, in respect to No. 34, Rabbi says Eliezer is a Shammaite; but a later authority states that in the very same manner Rabbi ruled according to Eliezer. This would seem to cancel out No. 34. Eliezer's alleged connection to the House of Shammai figures not at all in 120 of the approximately 130 pericopae. To be sure, the Houses themselves are concentrated in only part of the same sections of law. But Eliezer's and the Houses' laws center upon agricultural, Sabbath-festival, and uncleanness law, so the possibilities for alleging Eliezer to have been a Shammaite greatly outnumber the actual instances of such allegations. In all one can hardly say the view that Eliezer was a Shammaite figured in the Mishnah-Toseftan stratum or consistently played a role in the formulation of the traditions before ca. 250.

Apart from the stories which represent Eliezer as a sorcerer or a min, not a single item in the tradition can be called hostile to him or not respectful of his authority and traditions. But the sorcery-stories in the first instance involve Aqiba and Joshua, so we cannot take it as an effort to denigrate Eliezer as a sorcerer, unless we suppose that accepted into the tradition was a similar view of Aqiba -- whose students are ultimately responsible for the tradition. Hence it seems unlikely that the materials of Tos. Sanh. are so formulated as to reflect a hostile view of Eliezer. The min-stories are similarly told in a way respectful of Eliezer's authority. He is represented as having made a serious mistake. The Hegemon says the moral of the story: What is a sage like you doing in a place like this? And since Eliezer is represented as shrewd enough to get himself acquitted, the story should not be regarded as different in spirit from all that have come before it.

CHAPTER FIVE
THE ELIEZER OF HISTORY

i. Introduction

Having distinguished the more from the less useful traditions, we now seek to recover the picture of Eliezer drawn by his contemporaries and immediate disciples. That picture is composed of what several individuals who ought to have known what they were talking about said about Eliezer either in the course of his lifetime or shortly after his death. Our assumption is that those individuals or circles were not in collusion, but approached the Eliezer-materials from varying perspectives. Their sayings and stories, handed on in different ways to different circles, produce points of agreement among disparate authorities which allow us to construct a reasonably reliable account of the historical Eliezer. They further permit us to raise questions, not necessarily elicited by Eliezer's actual sayings, about his place in the larger historical setting. We shall rapidly review the positive results of an inquiry into the best and better traditions and then use those results to answer a number of questions.

ii. Topics of the Law

1. Agricultural Rules, Tithes, and Taboos

One may give Heave-offering from what is clean for what is unclean, and Dough-offering from clean for unclean dough. To prevent abuse of the rule, one may not give worse produce (unclean) for better (clean), for this would diminish the return to the priests. The established rule, to which Eliezer takes exception, however, rigidly distinguishes among various sorts of closely related produce or of the same produce in different states, i.e., liquids and solids. In permitting an exception to the rule, Eliezer made it considerably less complicated to give the requisite produce. He stands close to the position of the House of Shammai, which ruled that if a man gave Heave-offering of grapes intended for eating but later on made them into raisins, it is valid Heave-offering, and the gift does not have to be duplicated.

If one has to burn Heave-offering of hames that is clean with the same that is unclean, one must keep them separate. (Joshua says they may be burned together.)

With the Heave-offering which has fallen into a large quantity of secular produce, if one knows what has fallen into what, then one may not regard the Heave-offering as neutralized. But if one cannot distinguish the holy from the secular produce, the whole mixture will neutralize the Heave-offering. This is Meir's, and the Mishnah's, view of Eliezer's opinion on the matter. Judah places Eliezer in a still more lenient position. We may take for granted that Eliezer and Joshua discussed the principles of the neutralization of Heave-offering, but we are not entirely sure of Eliezer's exact opinion. Clearly, he took the lenient position vis à vis Joshua.

The cakes of Thank-offering and wafers of the Nazirite are not liable for Dough-offering if they are made for the Nazirite's own use, but are liable if made for sale.

'Orlah-laws do not apply outside of Palestine. We may generalize that the application of agricultural taboos is thereby suspended for foreign countries -- a major reform, if the rule was originated by Eliezer.

In respect to a hide anointed by Seventh Year oil, one may make use of it, and by extension one may use Seventh Year oil for that purpose. It is entirely legitimate to do so. The opposition held the hide should be burned -- and attributed that opinion to Eliezer. Eliezer wanted the enforcement of the laws of Seventh Year produce to be lenient. The same applies to the 'eruv, a law evidently unique to pre-70 Pharisaism. His rules would make it easy for non-Pharisees to take up the Pharisaic discipline, just as he (theoretically) removed that discipline from the concern of Jewries abroad.

One may not purchase saffron with the money of Second Tithe, because it is not a food, merely a coloring.

The etrog is like a tree in all respects, contrary to the view of Gamaliel that it is like a tree in three ways and like a vegetable in one.

2. Sabbaths and Festivals

One may do anything necessary for circumcision on the Sabbath. Aqiba ruled that on the Sabbath one may do only the thing which cannot be done before the Sabbath -- the actual act of circumcision itself. Conversely, in Eliezer's view, if one circumcizes on the Sabbath a child who does not have to be circumcised on that day, he will be liable for an appropriate Sin-offering.

However big a field, if it is surrounded by a fence it is regarded as a single domain and requires no 'eruv, and one may carry therein on the Sabbath. This is the most lenient possible ruling on the subject. Aqiba presents a stricter law. Likewise, if one party forgot to participate in the 'eruv for a courtyard, he is prohibited from using it, but all others in the courtyard may continue to do so, a lenient opinion which removes social pressure from the man who failed to participate in the rite, and, by extension, from the dissenter who does not believe in it to begin with. One may furthermore purchase a share in an 'eruv from a storekeeper or baker. The sages hold one may not do so by means of coins. One may make an 'eruv with any kind of food except water and salt. Joshua says it has to be a loaf of bread only. These are consistent with Eliezer's general leniency in regard to the 'eruv in particular, and Sabbath-law in general.

The 'Powers of Rain' prayer is said from the first day of Sukkot. A Sukkah must have some sort of a roof. One may carry out his obligation to consume bitter herbs on Passover by eating an herb which others regarded as not appropriate -- evidently a lenient opinion. Judah in the name of Eliezer gives three rulings on the conduct of the Temple rite on the Day of Atonement: how the high priest drew lots, where he would stand, and how he would count as he sprinkled the blood. Eliezer held, consistent with the House of Hillel, that one may make use of a splinter with which to pick his teeth on the festival, even though the wood was not set aside for that purpose before the festival. One may set up a new millstone in the festival week. A woman may go out on the Sabbath wearing a tiara.

3. Family Affairs

Eliezer greatly facilitated annulling vows. One may release a man from his vow by referring to the honor of his parents. Saddoq drew the conclusion that, if so, one may do so also with reference to the honor of God, and so vows are no longer going to be effective. One may release a man from his vow even by reason of what happens unexpectedly. Saddoq certainly would have to point out that vows can never again be taken seriously, for on any pretext whatever they may be rendered null and void.

A female minor can do nothing of legal effect. Eliezer therefore would rule out the possibility of the marriage of a minor under any circumstances.

A conditional writ of divorce, permitting a woman to marry anyone except one particular person, is valid. This ruling limits a woman's freedom in the situation of divorce. It is more or less consistent with Eliezer's view that one is obligated to carry out the rite of the Sotah if he has any reason whatever -- any sort of evidence satisfies Eliezer -- to suspect that she has been unfaithful. It is likewise consistent with his opinion that a woman is not to study Torah, but that her sole occupation should be home-making. Eliezer's view of divorce with a limiting condition may be regarded as parallel to the opinion of the House of Hillel, that any sort of grounds will justify a divorce. But it is not a close parallel, and distinctions between the two rulings may easily be introduced. A writ of divorce brought from one village to another -- not merely from a foreign country -- must have the verification of the agent that in his presence the writ was written and sealed. One warns his wife in regard to the Sotah-rite on the evidence of a single witness or on his own evidence, but causes her to drink on the evidence of two -- or the opposite.

4. Theoretical Problems

If a person has begun a deed licitly, he may complete it, even though in the meantime it is no longer permitted to undertake such an action.

Eliezer rules in a lenient way on the possibility of restoring to their original condition mixtures of sacred and secular substances. If a se'ah of unclean Heave-offering fell into a large quantity of clean, it may be removed, "for I say, the se'ah which fell in is the one which is lifted out." Likewise in a mixture of valid Whole-offering limbs with those which were blemished, if the head of one is offered, the others are all acceptable, because the one which was offered is assumed to be that of the blemished animal; the rest are thereby rendered valid. If various sacrificial bloods are mixed together, it is possible to sprinkle them. The sages say the whole has to be poured out, which will require a new sacrifice.

On the question of intent, Eliezer says that outside of the cult one judges only from what one actually does, rather than attempting to work out a person's intent without an explicit statement of what he actually proposed to do. Joshua says one may indeed interpret a man's intention. Eliezer's view of the problem of intention is consistent with opinion of the House of Shammai, that unstated intention is not taken into account in assessing the effect of a person's actions. The wrong intention, however, can render a sacred act or cultic object invalid. Thus if a man intended to do something wrong with the handful of the Meal-offering, whether or not he actually carried out his intention, he has rendered the offering invalid. If a man intended to eat something not ordinarily eaten or do something improper with a sacrifice, he has invalidated it. In respect to Sin-offering-water, the wrong intention, without any action, will render the water unfit. Joshua says not the intention but the actual action is what will render the water unfit. Likewise a sacrifice must be offered only for the purpose for which it may appropriately be designated, thus with exactly the right intention. If one sacrifices on the Passover coinciding with the Sabbath an animal eligible for the Passover sacrifice, but for a purpose other than the Passover, he is liable for a Sin-offering. This is the converse of Eliezer's view that one may actually do all that is needed in connection with such a sacrifice: One must be sure that the sacrifical process is absolutely required. Similarly in respect to the circumcision necessary on the Sabbath, one may do all the required preparations on that day; but if the circumcision is not necessarily done on the Sabbath, then Eliezer will rule in a strict way as to the appropriate penalty. One must do the right thing in the right way with the correct intention. Joshua says doing the right thing is sufficient, even with the wrong intention. The case of the Passover underlines the view of Eliezer that for sacrifices and the cult in general one's intention must be fully and correctly spelled out.

Eliezer and Aqiba, Eliezer and Joshua, and Eliezer and Judah b. Batyra are represented in three unrelated cases as disputing the identical legal principle, namely, whether a man must exert himself to forestall the development of an illegal situation, or whether he may simply stand by while such a situation takes shape on its own. Judah b. Batyra is of the same view as Eliezer. Joshua and Aqiba both differ from Eliezer; the differences are in separate pericopae. One should undertake no action which will produce a violation of the law. Therefore, in giving Dough-offering on the fifteenth of Nisan, a woman should not designate the offering until the dough is baked. Joshua says she should not worry about the problem of leaven on Passover in this connection. One therefore has, according to Eliezer, to take affirmative action in order to avoid violating the law. Joshua says one needs to do nothing, one way or the other; if the law is broken of itself, that is no one's problem. Eliezer likewise rules in respect to a mixture of blood to be sprinkled once with blood to be sprinkled four times that one must sprinkle the whole four times, lest he diminish the required number of sprinklings and so violate the law. Joshua says one should do no such thing; he should sprinkle just once.

5. The Theory of the Cult

If one does many individual transgressions of a single category in a single period of unawareness, he must bring a Sin-offering for each transgression. Aqiba says one Sin-offering suffices for all such acts. Aqiba on the one side, and Joshua and Gamaliel on the other, all are involved with the issue of how to atone for several actions of the same sort done in the same spell of unawareness. Joshua, Gamaliel, and Eliezer respond to the issue. Gamaliel and Joshua say they have no tradition. Eliezer supplies a ruling based upon logic. Then Gamaliel and Joshua cite an appropriate case which turns out to accord with the conclusion produced by Eliezer's logic. A man also must give a Sin-offering when he is not certain just what sin he has done, when he has done it, or indeed whether he has sinned at all. If the Sin-offering is not for the sin the man thinks he might have done, it will serve for some other. Similarly, one may bring a Suspensive Guilt-offering every day except for the day after the Day of Atonement.

6. The Temple and Sacrifice

One may dedicate to the Temple part of his property, but not all of it. Eliezer and Joshua rule on the question of what to do with a man who has dedicated his property to the Temple while liable for his wife's Ketuvah, but we are not sure exactly what each authority stated in such a case.

If a person has set aside a redemption-lamb for the firstling of an ass, the owner is liable for that lamb and must make it up if it dies. The sages say the owner is not liable to restore the lamb. Joshua and Saddoq support the latter position. The progeny of Peace-offerings may not be brought as Peace-offerings. Joshua and Pappyas have a tradition that the progeny may be given as Peace-offerings.

The 'blood without the meat' is ineffectual. That is, if the sprinkling of the blood has been carried out, but the sacrifice itself is proved to be impaired, the whole thing must be done again. Aqiba says the opposite also is the case. According to Eliezer, however, if the proper sprinkling of the blood does not take place, then the meat is not retrospectively rendered unfit.

If one slaughters at night and in the morning finds the walls of the neck filled with blood, the slaughter is valid.

7. Sources of Uncleanness

Joshua and Eliezer debate the definition of liquids which are capable of becoming unclean and rendering produce susceptible to uncleanness. We are not certain about the exact details of the discussion.

Eliezer says the sap of crushed olives is not capable of receiving or rendering susceptible to uncleanness.

Eliezer and Joshua deal with the case of two jars, each containing a half-olive's bulk of corpse, which are stopped up. In a house they together serve to render the house unclean. But the jars themselves are clean. If one is open, it and the house are unclean, the other remaining clean. Judah refines the dispute. Eliezer and Joshua likewise discuss the case in which an olive's bulk of corpse cleaves to the outer Joshua of the door jamb of the threshhold. Eliezer says it renders the house unclean. Joshua says the house remains clean. An olive's bulk of flesh from the limb of a living person is unclean. The dirt of a grave area and that which comes from abroad join together to make up the quantity capable of rendering something unclean. The sages say that quantity can be composed only of a single sort of dirt -- therefore a lenient rule.

8. Persons Subject to Ritual Uncleanness

If a person deliberately removed the tokens of uncleanness in respect to an attack of leprosy, he can become clean only after the purification of another sign of leprosy which afterward occurs on his flesh. Judah b. Ilai claims Eliezer and the sages hold that such a person can never be purified. They differ as to one who cut off the sign as dead flesh.

If a Nazir contracts uncleanness at the very end of his spell, he need not lose the whole of the period he has already properly observed. He loses only a small part of the period.

A Zab who examined himself only on the first and seventh days of his period is regarded as having been clean on the intermediate days, a lenient ruling.

9. Objects Subject to Ritual Uncleanness

A shoe on the last is insusceptible to uncleanness, because it is not completed. This represents the application of an old principle to a new case. The beehive will save from uncleanness what is in an earthenware vessel, since it has the capacity to preserve its contents from severe corpse-uncleanness. The sages hold that partitions afford protection in a 'Tent,' but not in earthenware vessels; considerations of logic do not change the situation. Eliezer proposes to extend by logic an established decision, and the sages stand pat. A beehive is like immovable property. The sages hold the opposite opinion. A money-bag or a pouch for pearls is unclean. We are not sure which object was subject to Eliezer's ruling. When broken, a metal vessel may both contract uncleanness and be rendered clean. Eliezer rules on whether a handkerchief, a wrapper for a Torah-scroll, and a towel are subject to the law of diverse kinds, but we do not know what he said. Judah claims he said they are not subject to the taboo.

10. The Courts

A pigeon-racer may not give testimony. A woman is covered up before her body is hung.

11. The Schools

One must repeat a lesson to his disciple four times. Aqiba said one must do so as many times as are necessary for the disciple to master the tradition.

12. The Age

The generation of the wilderness is destined to enjoy the world to come. Aqiba denies it.

iii. Origins, Early Life, Education

We do not know where Eliezer came from, who his parents were, how he was educated, at what point in life he became a Pharisee, whom he married, when or where he died. The historical Eliezer lacks a personal biography. But the information in our hands permits a number of likely surmises.

First, he certainly was a Pharisee. The topics of his best-attested legal rulings leave no doubt on that question, for they focus upon the two areas of everyday life -- agricultural taboos and ritual purity -- which constitute the primary interests of Pharisaism. The third important interest in his legislation, the cult, follows from the first two. The Pharisees before 70 did not control the Temple and did not make laws to govern its cult. But afterward, they made plans for the conduct of the Temple when it would be restored. The reason for their strong interest in the matter was that their piety had earlier centered upon the priesthood, cult, and Temple; they had stressed the proper provision of the priestly taxes -- though they did not necessarily benefit -- and the appropriate, domestic application of the purity-laws of the Temple. It therefore was important to Eliezer, as a representative of pre-70 Pharisaism, to continue the earlier trend to make laws affecting the governance of the cultic life. Nothing in Eliezer's legal legacy suggests that he anticipated the Temple would be subordinated in the spirituality of his day or later times; nothing replaced the offerings, no one took the place of the priest, no new forms of piety were evolved to substitute for those that had depended upon the Temple's sanctity.

Among the Yavnean authorities ought to have been others not likely to have been Pharisees before 70 -- priests, Sadducees, apocalyptics and mystics, adherents of other groups, rich men, common folk. We need not doubt that Gamaliel was a Pharisee, for his father, Simeon, is explicitly named as one by Josephus, and his grandfather, Gamaliel, is likewise so characterized by Acts' version of Paul. But Simeon's daughter married a disciple of Yohanan b. Zakkai said not to have been a Pharisee; it is difficult to demonstrate that Yohanan himself was a member of the sect before 70. His legal rulings hardly supply decisive evidence that he was, Eliezer's do.

Second, he probably was born and educated before the destruction of Jerusalem. On this question we can be less certain. It is only an assumption, based on the surviving materials, that Eliezer, along with Joshua, Gamaliel, Saddoq, Tarfon, and a few others, constituted the first group of important Yavnean authorities, after Yohanan himself. If this assumption is sound, then Eliezer, among the others, presumably was a mature man at the beginning of the Yavnean period. He certainly was well informed about Pharisaic law, so probably learned it before 70.

This must mean, third, that before 70 he was inducted into the sect. We do not know how the Pharisees taught neophytes, though the legal traditions on the subject are clear that a gradual process of absorption marked entry into the sect. The beginner was taught simple, then more complex rules; he began by tithing, then went on to the larger and more difficult matter of learning to preserve the ritual purity of secular food. But whether this process was carried out by formal education, discipleship or in some other way is hardly clear. Nor do we have evidence of his education in other subjects, such as philosophy, science, mysticism, or Greek language, not to mention Scripture and other sacred subjects. To be sure, much may be taken for granted about the education of any

Jewish male in first-century Palestine, for knowledge of Scriptures -- but what books and in what recensions who can say? -- and the rites and liturgy of the country's Jews may be presumed to have been widespread. But we find in the traditions pertinent to the historical Eliezer no information whatever about educational institutions, curricula, techniques, or goals.

Fourth, he certainly does not appear to have been a priest or a Levite. Nothing in his sayings indicates much interest in priestly or Levitical affairs as such, apart from those aspects that impinged upon the Pharisaic piety.

We know nothing about the master whom he might have served as a disciple or whether he was part of a master-disciple circle at all. Nothing in the materials before us permits speculation about his station of life, his personal wealth, his family's occupation, his class sympathies. His personal traits are revealed, if the saying is genuine, only by the counsel to repent before death -- a commonplace of the time, meant to inculcate not a morbid spirit but ethical behavior.

If his view that the generation of the wilderness will enjoy the world to come means more than it says, then Eliezer also believed in the power not only of penitence but also of divine grace. This belief does not imply personality-traits of one kind or another. But it does permit the guess that in his time the issues of penitence and grace were important. This, to be sure, we might have surmised without such a saying, for with the destruction of the Temple, it was natural for people to speculate about reconciliation with God and its means -- penitence on man's side, grace on God's.

iv. Eliezer's Active Career

We do not know where Eliezer lived in the years after 70 or what he did for a living. We do not know much about how he spent his time, though the legal record requires the surmise that he gave great effort to legal study and legislation. He was associated in this connection chiefly with Joshua and Aqiba, secondarily with Gamaliel and Saddoq, and practically not at all with other important masters of his own day. Ilai has legal traditions in his name, so Eliezer presumably taught Ilai as a disciple, but we do not know for what purpose -- whether to train him for a career in public administration or merely to educate him as an observant Pharisee. The latter would seem more likely; the bulk of Ilai's chains have to do with religious observance, not the administration of justice, on which, from Eliezer, we have almost no sayings.

The best traditions make one thing clear: at some point in his life Eliezer fell under a shadow, so that it was necessary to preserve his traditions in a peculiar way -- by saying he said the opposite of what was his true opinion. It was difficult for Ilai to find others to verify that Eliezer had said what his best disciple had as the record of his teaching. We do not know what happened. Since the two lists of evidently controversial teachings place Eliezer in a lenient vis à vis Pharisaic law, it stands to reason that he had proposed a considerable revision of earlier Pharisaism. This revision would have included a lenient approach to the application of the 'eruv-laws and of the laws on the Seventh Year. It further involved a rapproachment with the Samaritans -- not a matter of concern only to Pharisees. According to him, Jews might now enter social relations with Samaritans.

The revision of Eliezer's traditions by Aqiba therefore reflects some public event which changed the relationship between Eliezer and the larger body of the sages. His opinions were no longer acceptable. Then Aqiba, who agreed with Eliezer's views, claimed in Eliezer's name the exact opposite of what he had originally said so as to secure the acceptance of his opinions. Ilai had the same problem, but he simply preserved the traditions as best he could. He hoped to find others who might support his allegation of Eliezer's real opinion and perhaps also testify that these should be the normative law. Ilai's list of lenient rulings of Eliezer had to do with 'eruv-laws and a bitter herb for Passover. But while he was unable to find others who knew equivalent lenient rulings in Eliezer's name, his list was preserved in the appropriate context. Aqiba's little list of traditions in Eliezer's name, which contained lenient rulings in respect to the Seventh Year -- one may use a hide anointed with the oil of the Seventh Year, and in regard to the relationships with Samaritans -- one may have social intercourse with them ("eat their bread"), likewise was preserved. At some point both traditions were taken into the normative compilations, so in time the reasons for suppressing them ceased to be important or were forgotten. I should suppose this came with the predominance of Aqiba's disciples, at Usha. But we must also postulate that Ishmael, who clearly disapproved of Eliezer's teachings, must have stood among Eliezer's opposition. His virtual absence from Eliezer's corpus, rather than anything he actually is claimed to have said, represents the best evidence of the state of affairs. Eliezer's pericopae place him in relationships chiefly with Joshua and Aqiba, so his disciples and theirs are apt to be responsible for the formation of the larger part of the corpus of the best and -- it goes without saying -- the better traditions. That is why we have them. Perhaps the reason for Aqiba's favorable attitude toward Eliezer is what the later stories allege: he was Eliezer's disciple. But Joshua's place is much less clear. We cannot take for granted that Joshua and Eliezer studied with the same master; on the contrary, if they had, they should have stood together on a wide range of moot issues. It seems more likely that they were associated because they shared a common agendum of legal concerns and differed on minor details, indicating a broad range of agreement on fundamental principles.

Of other alleged disciples of Yohanan b. Zakkai we hear nothing at all. Simeon b. Natanel was married to Gamaliel's daughter; Eliezer was married to his sister. So the two should have come in contact. We have no evidence of that fact. Yosi the Priest is quite unheard of in Eliezer's (or others') traditions. Eleazar b. 'Arakh, a mystic, plays no role whatever. Among contemporaries, Tarfon and Eleazar b. 'Azariah seem important. The former is supposed to have been another teacher of Aqiba, the latter is given an important place in the consistory of Gamaliel. Saddoq comes in chiefly through Joshua, with whom he is repeatedly associated, though he has some independent sayings or interpolations as well. In all, therefore, the traditions about Eliezer place him into close relationships with the figures of greatest importance in the surviving materials of early Yavnean times.

v. Eliezer's Historical Situation. Pharisaism and Rabbinism

We do not know where Eliezer spent the years before the War of 66 or how he reached Yavneh. Nor have we evidence on his attitude to either the War of 66 or war in general. He cannot certainly be called either a nationalist and zealot or a pacifist. We do know that in his time the Temple was destroyed. His attitude toward the destruction of the Temple is not difficult to recover. He clearly devoted his best energies to working out the laws of the Temple cult, so he believed in the cult and presumably regretted the Temple's destruction and the consequent cessation of animal sacrifices. The cultic rules obviously are matters of legal theory; they do not derive from Eliezer's actual knowledge of how the Temple had been run before 70, nor do they indicate much interest in the question. Precedents are seldom cited in Eliezer's discussions. To be sure, he has a number of sayings about the conduct of the cult on the Day of Atonement; these are matters of generally unimportant detail and do not add up to much.

Clearly, Eliezer expected the Temple to be rebuilt. Since he made up laws for the rebuilt sanctuary, he presumably wanted to see the reconstruction and anticipated that in the new Temple his laws would be enforced. Hence he believed in the efficacy of the cult and did not doubt it would be restored. We have no hint that he disapproved of the former Temple. The absence of traditions on that subject is because he was not a priest and had no clear knowledge of what had been done. When he did, he gave it -- that much emerges from Judah's sayings in his name. So presumably he thought what had been done in general should be repeated in the future, with modification of details. These he figured out on the basis of logic. His concern for the Temple marks him once again as a Pharisee, for, as stated, Pharisaic piety was based upon the Temple and its laws of uncleanness; the Pharisees simply enlarged the area in which those laws were to be observed and enforced. Whether or not they liked the particular Temple administration, the Pharisees certainly revered the cult itself and took most seriously the laws surrounding its conduct, including, first and foremost, purity laws. Later on the cult and its law would be considerably less interesting, in particular to generations entirely unfamiliar with its appeal. The theory of the cult, to be sure, would occupy the lawyers for a long time to come.

In Eliezer's time Rome ended its former experiments with the government of the Jews and established direct rule. We know nothing about Eliezer's attitude toward Rome and the new regime in Palestine. Gamaliel had to negotiate with it; Eliezer evidently did not. This must mean that in Yavneh he did not enter into direct relationships with the Roman regime; but we do not know whether other masters of the day, except for Gamaliel, had any more direct contact with the Romans than he evidently did.

The larger problems faced by the Jews deprived of their cult and its celebrations, including the observance in the Temple and in Jerusalem of the pilgrim-festivals, not to mention the bringing of first fruits and of the Second Tithes or equivalent funds to the city of consumption -- none of these seem to have elicited his attention. He does not legislate about the observance of Sukkot after the destruction, as did Yohanan b. Zakkai, though we have two rulings pertinent to the festival. He has nothing to say about the New Year or the use of the shofar on the Sabbath that coincides with the New Year, as did

Yohanan; also omitted are the use of new produce and the waving of the 'omer. The various Temple-oriented festival celebrations subject to Yohanan's taqqanot are ignored in Eliezer's legislation. This is striking, for Eliezer, as an early Yavnean master, ought to have had more to say about the sacred rites now no longer possible to effect than we can discern in respect to these lively issues.

Eliezer certainly did not anticipate that the Temple would never be rebuilt. He had no program for any considerable time before the reconstruction. Perhaps it was hoped that the Romans would not delay in permitting the buildings to be restored. No one in his time could foresee the disastrous Bar Kokhba War or the definitive prohibition of the Jews from Jerusalem in its aftermath.

Eliezer's legislation therefore suggests he presumed life would soon go on pretty much as it had in the past. Issues important to pre-70 Pharisaism predominate in his laws; issues absent in the rabbinic traditions about the Pharisees are -- except the cult -- mostly absent in his as well. Eliezer therefore comes at the end of the old Pharisaism, not the beginning of a new rabbinism -- traces of which are quite absent in his historically usable traditions. Indeed, on the basis of his laws and sayings we can hardly define what this rabbinism might consist of. The centrality of the Oral Torah, the view of the rabbi as the new priest and of study of Torah as the new cult, the conception of piety as the imitation of Moses "our rabbi" and the conception of God as a rabbi, the organization of the Jewish community under rabbinic rule and by rabbinic law, and the goal of turning all Israel into a vast academy for the study of the (rabbinic) Torah -- none of these motifs characteristic of latter rabbinism occurs at all. Since by the end of the Yavnean period the main outlines of rabbinism were clear, we may postulate that the transition from Pharisaism or rabbinism or the union of the two took place in the time of Eliezer himself. But he does not seem to have been among those who generated the new viewpoints; he appears as a reformer of the old ones. His solution to the problem of the cessation of the cult was not to replace the old piety with a new one, but rather to preserve and refine the rules governing the old in the certain expectation of its restoration in a better form than ever. Others, who were his contemporaries and successors, developed the rabbinic idea of the (interim) substitution of study for sacrifice, the rabbi for the priest, and the Oral Torah of Moses "our rabbi" for the piety of the old cult.

Indeed, the virtual absence of rabbinic ideas not only among the best and better traditions, but even among the poorest ones, shows, as observed, that Eliezer has not been anachronistically 'rabbinized.' To be sure, the tradents and compilers later on assumed everyone before them -- back to Moses -- was a rabbi. But they did not regularly attribute to Eliezer sayings to link him specifically to the rabbinic system of symbols, and this suggests that, just as with the laws, a limited agendum defined topics appropriate for attribution to Eliezer, so with theological matters, ideas originally not within Eliezer's agendum were not commonly added afterward. If so, we may take seriously the attribution of rabbinic ideas to others of his contemporaries. Where do we first find them?

Clearly Yohanan b. Zakkai -- whom we cannot conclusively show to have been a Pharisee -- appears to have been a rabbi. It is in his sayings, admittedly first occurring in

86 The Problem of the Attributed Saying

late compilations, that we find the claim of replacing the cult with something -- anything -- as good. He is alleged to have told Joshua that deeds of loving kindness achieve atonement, just as did the cult. He is further made to say that man was created in order to study the Torah. When Israel does the will of their father in heaven -- which is contained in the Torah and taught by the rabbi -- then no nation or race can rule over them. The cult is hardly central to his teachings and seldom occurs in his laws. The altar to be sure serves to make peace between Israel and the father in heaven -- but is not so important ("how much the more so") as a man who makes peace among men or is a master of Torah. Yohanan's taqqanot are even better testimony, for they take account of the end of the cult and provide for the period of its cessation. The Temple rites may be carried on ("as a memorial") outside of the old sanctuary. The old priesthood is subjected to the governance of the rabbi. The priest had to pay the sheqel and ideally should marry anyone the rabbi declares to be a fit wife. Eliezer says nothing of the sort; what Yohanan has to say about the situation after 70 is either without parallel in Eliezer's sayings or contradicted by their tendency. To be sure, we are scarcely able to claim that rabbinism begins with Yohanan or that Pharisaism ends with Eliezer. But Yohanan's tradition certainly reveals the main theological themes of later rabbinism -- though these themes are more reliably attributed to later Yavneans and still more adequately spelled out in their sayings. And Eliezer's laws and theological sayings are strikingly silent about what later on would be the primary concern of the rabbinic authorities, the Oral Torah in all its social and political ramifications, and remarkably narrow in their focus upon the concerns of pre-70 Pharisaism.

Further investigation may show that the list of M. Avot of Yohanan's disciples represents a composite of the five components of the Yavnean group: Eliezer clearly was a Pharisee; Yosi was a priest; Simeon b. Nathaniel was an 'am ha'ares, not observant of the purity laws; Eleazar b. 'Arakh was a mystic; and Joshua b. Hananiah should represent rabbinism. But this remains to be studied.

If Eliezer stands for the Old Pharisaism, who stands for the scribes? The scribes form a distinct group -- not merely a profession -- in the Gospels' account of Jesus's opposition. Scribes and Pharisees are not regarded as one and the same group. To be sure, what scribes say and do not say is not made clear. One cannot derive from the Synoptic record a clear picture of scribal doctrine, if any, though one certainly finds an account of the Pharisaic law on ritual uncleanness and tithing. Since the materials now found in the Synoptics certainly were available in Palestine between 70 and 90, however, they may be presumed accurately to portray the situation of that time, because their picture had to be credible to Christians of the period. (Even the Fourth Gospel contains traditions that go back to Palestine before 70, but we concentrate attention on the picture presented by the Synoptics.) If so, we have in the Synoptics a portrait of two groups at Yavneh (and possibly earlier) in close relationship with one another, but not entirely unified.

Now, having seen in Eliezer an important representative of the old Pharisaism, we find no difficulty in accounting for the Pharisaic component of the Yavnean situation. It likewise seems reasonable to locate in the Scribes the antecedents of the ideological or symbolic part of the rabbinic component at Yavneh. Admittedly, our information on scribism in the rabbinic literature is indistinguishable from the later sayings produced by rabbinism. But if we consider that scribism goes back to much more ancient times than does Pharisaism, with its main outlines clearly represented, for instance, by Ben Sira, we may suppose that what the scribe regarded as the center of piety was study, interpretation and application of the Torah. To be sure, what was studied and how it was interpreted are not to be identified with the literature and interpretation of later rabbinism. But the scribal piety and the rabbinic piety are expressed through an identical symbol, Torah. And one looks in vain in the rabbinic traditions about the Pharisees before 70 for stress on, or even the presence of the ideal of, the study of Torah. Unless rabbinism begins as the innovation of the early Yavneans -- and this seems to me unlikely -- it should represent at Yavneh the continuation of pre-70 scribism.

But it continued with an important difference, for Yavnean and later rabbinism said what cannot be located in pre-70 scribal documents: The Temple cult was replaced by study of Torah, the priest by the rabbi (= scribe); and the center of piety was shifted away from sacrifice entirely. So Yavnean scribism-rabbinism made important changes in pre-70 scribal ideas. It responded to the new situation in a more appropriate way than did Yavnean Pharisaism represented by Eliezer. Eliezer could conceive of no piety outside of that focused upon the Temple. But Yavnean and late scribism-rabbinism was able to construct an expression of piety which did not depend upon the Temple at all. Eliezer appears as a reformer of old Pharisaism; the proponents of rabbinism do not seem to have reformed old scribism. What they did was to carry the scribal ideal to its logical conclusion. If study of Torah was central and knowledge of Torah important, then the scribe had authority even in respect to the Temple and the cult; indeed, his knowledge was more important than what the priest knew. This view, known in the sayings of Yohanan b. Zakkai, himself an opponent of the priesthood in Yavnean times, is not a matter only of theoretical consequence. Yohanan also held that he might dispose of Temple practices and take them over for the Yavnean center -- and for other places as well -- and so both preserve them ("as a memorial") and remove from the Temple and the priests a monopoly over the sacred calendar, festivals, and rites. Earlier scribism thus contained within itself the potentiality to supersede the cult. It did not do so earlier, because it had no reason to, and because it probably could not. The later rabbinism, faced with the occasion and the necessity, realized that potentiality. By contrast, earlier Pharisaism invested its best energies in the replication of the cult, not in its replacement. After 70 it could do no more than plan for its restoration.

Scribism as an ideology, not merely a profession, begins with the view that the law given by God to Moses was binding and therefore has to be interpreted and applied to daily affairs. That view must go back to the fourth century B.C., by which time Nehemiah's establishment of the Torah of Moses as the constitution of Judea had to have produced important effects in ordinary life. From that time on those who could authoritatively apply the Torah constituted an important profession. The writings of scribes stress the identification of Torah with wisdom and the importance of learning. Ben Sira's sage travels widely in search of wisdom and consorts with men of power. Into the first century, the scribes must have continued as in identifiable estate, high in the country's administration. Otherwise the Synoptics' view is incomprehensible. So those who were professionally acquainted with the Scriptures -- whether they were priests or not -- formed an independent class of biblical teachers, lawyers, administrators, or scribes, alongside the priesthood. We do not know what they actually did in the administration of the country. Perhaps Yohanan b. Zakkai's reference to decrees of Jerusalem authorities (M. Ket. 13:1ff.) alludes to the work of scribes, who therefore were involved -- as the Pharisees certainly were not -- in the determination of family law and in the settlement of trivial disputes.

The NT references support this supposition. The scribes occur in association with the high priests in Matt. 2:4, 16:21, 20:18, 21:15, 27, 27:41, Mk. 8:31, 10:33, 11:18, 27; 14:1, 43, 53; 15:1, 31, etc.; with the Pharisees in Mt. 5:20, 12:38, 15:1, 23:2, 13, ff.; Mk. 2:16, 7:1, 5. But they are not the same as the one or the other. The scribes are called 'learned in the law' and jurists (Matt. 22:35, Luke 7:30, 10:25, 11:45, 52, 14:3). They are teachers of the law (Luke 5:17, Acts 5:34).

Mishnaic literature -- except Eliezer's saying in M. Sot. 9:15 -- obviously will miss the distinction between Pharisees and scribes, both of whom are regarded as HKMYM, sages. But we have no reason to suppose all scribes were Pharisees, any more than that all Pharisees were scribes. Indeed, as Schürer points out (A History of the Jewish People, etc., Division II, Vol. I, pp. 319f.)., "Inasmuch... as the 'scribes' were merely 'men learned in the law,' there must have been also Sadducaean scribes. For it is not conceivable that the Sadducees, who acknowledged the written law is binding, should have had among them none who made it their profession to study it. In fact those passages of the New Testament, which speak of scribes who were of the Pharisees (Mark 2:16, Luke 5:30, Acts 23:9) point also to the existence of Sadducaean scribes." The scribes therefore represent a class of men learned in Scriptures, perhaps lawyers in charge of the administration of justice. They had to develop legal theory, teach pupils, and apply the law.

Naturally, such people would come to the center of the administration of government and law, so they could not have remained aloof from Yavneh. Some of them may, to be sure, have come because they were Pharisees. But others, whatever their original ritual practices, would have come because Yavneh represented the place in which they might carry on their profession.

The latter rabbinic history of the Second Temple assigns to the scribes the period from Ezra to Simeon the Just -- that is, the period before the (imaginary) existence of Pharisaism itself. It assumes of course that all scribes were Pharisees and all Pharisees were scribes, so it need not set aside a "scribal period" after Simeon, from whose time it traces the history of the Pharisaic-rabbinic party itself.

Josephus -- himself a new adherent of the Pharisees -- does not confuse the scribes with the Pharisees. In none of his allusions to the Pharisees does he also refer to the scribes (grammateis). In Life 197-8, he refers to a delegation of Jerusalemites to

Galilee. Two were from the lower ranks of society and adherents of the Pharisees, the third was also a Pharisee, but a priest; the fourth was descended from high priests. These were all able to assert that they were not ignorant of the customs of the fathers. To be sure, the Pharisees are referred to as knowledgeable in the Torah; and they have traditions from the fathers, in addition to those that Moses had revealed. But they are not called scribes. They were (War 1: 107-114) exact exponents of the laws. They also were (War 2: 162-166) the most accurate interpreters of the laws. But they are not called scribes. The long 'philosophical school' account in Antiquities 18: 11-17 describes the Pharisees as virtuous and says that "all prayers and sacred rites of divine worship are performed according to their exposition" -- but they too are not scribes.

When Josephus does refer to scribes, he does not refer to Pharisees. For example, in War 1: 648ff. = Antiquities 17: 152, he refers to two sophistai who ordered their disciples to pull down the eagle that Herod had set up in the Temple. They are Judah son of Sepphoraeus and Matthias son of Margalus, men who gave lectures on the laws, attended by a large, youthful audience. If these are scribes, they are not said also to be Pharisees, who do not occur in the account. We find also hierogrammateis and patrion exegetai nomon -- not in the context of the passages about the Pharisees. While, therefore, the Pharisees and the scribes have in common knowledge of the country's laws, the two are treated separately. Josephus does not regard the scribes as wholly within the Pharisaic group; he presents the scribe as a kind of authority or professional teacher of law. Josephus's further references to grammateus (sing. or pl.) are as follows:

> Apion 1:290: The sacred scribe Phritobeuates; Antiquities 6: 120: It was reported to the kind by the scribes that the host were sinning against God; 7: 110: He made Seisa scribe; 7: 293 = 7: 110; 7: 219: Joab took the chiefs of the tribes and scribes and took the census; 7: 364: David appointed six thousand Levites as judges of the people and as scribes; 9: 164: When the scribe and priest of the treasury had emptied the chest; 10: 55: When the money was brought, he gave superintendence of the temple... to the governor of the city [and] Sapha the scribe, etc.; 10: 94f.: Baruch, son of Jeremiah; 10: 149: the scribe of Sacchais; 11: 22, 26, 29: Semelios the scribe, etc.; 11: 128: On the scribes of the sanctuary you will impose no tribute; 12: 142: The scribes of the Temple; 11: 248, 250, 272, 287: scribes of the Persian kings; 16: 319: the scribe Diophantus had imitated his manner of writing; 20: 208f.: The sicarii kidnaped the secretary of the captain; War 1: 479: village clerks; 5: 532: Aristeus, the secretary of the council --

so H. Thackeray, Josephus Lexicon, Fascicle II, pp. 117-118. The entry for hierogrammateus is not yet [1972] available, nor for sophistes. It is clear, however, that Josephus does not associate scribes with Pharisees; no scribe is a Pharisee; and no Pharisee is described as a scribe. The two are separate and distinct. One is a sect, the other is a profession.

Since later rabbinism found pre-70 scribism highly congenial, it is by no means far-fetched to trace the beginnings of Yavnean rabbinism to the presence of representatives of the pre-70 scribal class, to whom the ideal of study of Torah rather than the piety of the cult and the replication of that cultic piety in one's own home, was central. Yavneh therefore incorporated these two important strands of pre-70 religion -- the one the piety of a sect, the other the professional ideal of a class -- and others as well. Among them, as we have seen, Eliezer's teachings made for pre-70 Pharisaism an important place in the Yavnean synthesis.

Thus far, our definition of rabbinism has focused upon its central symbols and ideas. These seem to continue symbols and ideas known, in a general way, from 'scribism' -- if not from individual scribes, who, as I have stressed, formed a profession, not a sect. But what of the later, and essential, characteristic trait of rabbinism, its formation as a well-organized and well-disciplined movement, its development of important institutions for the government of the Jewish communities of Palestine and Babylonia, its aspiration to make use of autonomous political instruments for the transformation of all Jews into rabbis? Of this, we have no knowledge at all in the earliest stratum of the Yavnean period. Clearly, Yohanan b. Zakkai worked out the relationship between the synagogue and the Temple. But the nature of the "gathering" at Yavneh -- whether it was some sort of 'academy,' or a nascent political institution, or merely an inchoate assembly of various sorts of sectarians, professionals, pre-70 authorities, and whatever -- is simply unilluminated. Eliezer's historical record is strikingly silent on this very point. From his materials we have no evidence on either how he enforced or applied the law outside of his own household or disciple-circle, or how anyone else did. We have no hint about the evolution of an institution one might regard as a nascent political authority -- a government -- in any terms. Eliezer's laws omit reference even to the legal theory behind such an authority. And they are strikingly silent about the whole range of laws to be applied in civil life. Whence such laws reached the Yavneans we do not know. They cannot have come from Eliezer, and, given the nature of the rabbinic traditions about pre-70 Pharisaism, they also did not derive from other Pharisees. So in all the 'rabbinism' possibly present in Yohanan's corpus and remarkably absent in Eliezer's is simply the symbolic and ideological element represented by the study of Torah as the central expression of piety.

vi. Eliezer's Own Contribution

The problem of what Eliezer himself contributed is important in helping to determine his larger policy for the reconstruction of Judaism after the destruction of the Temple. As is clear, it will not be easy to isolate his own laws from possibly earlier ones. It cannot be doubted, to be sure, that Eliezer assumed Pharisaism would continue as before. It would be a liberalized Pharisaism, with more cordial relations to the Samaritans, on the one side, and to the non-Pharisees, on the other. He evidently planned that observant Pharisees would enjoy more of the Seventh Year produce, and in more ways, than was hitherto deemed appropriate. Since these specific rulings were controversial, they were important, and others, we do not know who, so strongly rejected Eliezer's opinions that it became necessary to suppress even his name. But how serious an 'incident' was produced we cannot say; the bulk of the preserved traditions reveals no hostility or systematic opposition, and I assume there was none. It was the convention of rabbinic historiography to invent dramatic "incidents" out of the evidence of conflict, and so to represent as a clash of personalities what was originally a difference, of some seriousness to be sure, in matters of law. In the case of Eliezer the story was told that he had rejected the will of the majority and had preferred the opinion of Heaven; in the case of Gamaliel, his indifference to the poverty of the other sages and his disrespect for his colleagues were made into the occasion for his deposition. In both instances the stories follow long after the fact, which was, at least in respect to Eliezer, nowhere represented accurately, except in the laws.

All laws in Eliezer's name pertaining to the Temple are matters of legal theory and cannot have been enforced in Eliezer's time or afterward. But it is striking that other important sorts of law, for instance, tithing, agricultural taboos, and uncleanness rules, produce no evidence of how or even whether they were applied. In fact, on the basis of evidence before us we do not know that Eliezer exercised any kind of practical authority at all, except, possibly, in the matter of permitting circumcision on the Sabbath -- and this was in his own village. Nor does the evidence before us permit the description of the sort of institution -- whether civic or academic -- which Eliezer conducted (at Lydda?), the range of its authority, or the type of activity that took place within it. So far as we know, Eliezer's laws represented his own opinion, perhaps also that of other sages, but as to the nature of his and their authority after 70, we here have no information whatsoever. The later strata do not greatly change the situation, for only rarely do they even claim to supply evidence on Eliezer's practical activities, though they assume he applied the law as he taught it. In point of fact the considerable efforts on the part of Eliezer and others to preserve and reshape the Pharisaic law appear to have been chiefly, perhaps wholly, theoretical. If such was not the case, we are unable to demonstrate it.

But Eliezer's laws are strikingly silent about the sorts of public affairs that ought to have produced cases, precedents, and evidence that laws were enforced and how this was done. The most important kinds of law should have been civil law, torts and damages, conflicts over property, real estate litigations; criminal actions (unless the Jewish population produced no thieves, robbers, murderers, and the like, and this seems unlikely); the collection of taxes, the establishment of local courts and their conduct, including rules of evidence (on which we have one saying); practical Sabbath and festival law, involving questions other than whether one brings a Sin-offering to a non-existent Temple in the case of some minor violation; the application of the laws of family life, e.g., halisah (later on important in Babylonia), divorce-settlements, collection of the marriage-contract's specified dues; the rights of orphans and the division of estates; the regulation of the dietary laws observed by the bulk of the Jewish population (if there were numbers of such laws, and we cannot show that there were); and a wide range of similar, practical affairs. The sorts of laws which, for Babylonia, produced an abundance of cases are

virtually ignored in Eliezer's preserved corpus. This constitutes probative evidence that
Eliezer did not administer the affairs of the community and had no authority over them.
He contributed little, if at all, to the formulation of laws now codified in Neziqin and
much of Nashim as well as the practical tractates of Qodashim, Toharot (Niddah), and
much of Mo'ed, because, like earlier Pharisees, he had no traditions on these subjects and
now had no reason to deal with matters wholly outside the range of his practical authority
and concern. In no way, therefore, can Eliezer's civil authority be compared to that of a
later rabbi. Not only was his view of law purely Pharisaic, but so too was his conception
of its enforcement. His possibilities of carrying out even the trivial laws he thought
important were inconsequential. Whatever the situation of other Yavneans, Eliezer
cannot be seen as a political or a civil authority.

vii. Eliezer's Program for Yavneh

While we may trace the main outlines of Eliezer's plan for the interim-period in
which the cult would not be carried on, we are unable to show how, if at all, he effected
these plans. It presently would seem that they were matters of legal theory, without
practical consequence for the larger part of the Jewish population. That picture may
change with the detailed examination of traditions attributed to other contemporaries.
But it will not change for Eliezer himself, for it simply cannot be shown that he ever was
able to tell others what to do, nor have we evidence about the basis in practical politics
on which he might have attempted to take charge of the life of the larger community.

Perhaps his influence extended beyond the doors of his own house or the limits of his
own circles of disciples and like-minded colleagues. But we cannot show it and had best
not assume it. In point of fact whatever happened at Yavneh to yield evidence on the
practical effects of rabbinical administration of the life of the ordinary Jews leaves no
mark whatever on Eliezer's sayings. By contrast, while we do not know how Yohanan b.
Zakkai effected his Yavnean decrees -- if he carried them out at all -- at least the
substance of the decrees pertains to the life of common people. Eliezer legislated, in
theory if not in practice, primarily for people subject to Pharisaic discipline and mainly
about matters important to Pharisaic piety.

This fact underlines the conclusion already reached, that Eliezer's program for the
Yavnean period concerned Pharisaism and little else. We simply do not know what, if
anything, he might have had to say to non-Pharisaic Jews at Yavneh and in other parts of
the country. Perhaps the saying to repent before death then would have seemed more
important than it does now; but it hardly constitutes much of a program for a country
which had just lost its autonomous government and capital and a people suddenly without
a sanctuary or a cult.

In the aftermath of the destruction, Eliezer evidently intended to liberalize the
application of the Pharisaic discipline. I see no necessary connection between his intent
and the recent events. Perhaps he simply thought that by making it easier for large
numbers of Jews to take on the Pharisaic way of living, he might win over people who
aforetime were not Pharisees. Since, moreover, the Pharisaic laws enabled Jews outside

of the Temple to participate in its cult in their own homes and so as to share in its
sanctity, he may have posited the Pharisaic way as a means of preserving both the
sanctity and the symbolic presence of the cult during the interim in which they were no
more. Hence it may have seemed wise to formulate the Pharisaic laws in as lenient a way
as possible. But if this was Eliezer's intent -- and we cannot show that it certainly was --
I doubt his motive was purely propagandistic. He gives no evidence that his interest was
to win as many Jews as possible to the Pharisaic way and by subterfuge to make it easier
for them to undertake the sect's discipline. It is inconceivable to me that he stated a law
contrary to his real opinion merely to make it more acceptable to outsiders.

The main outlines of his policy for the present age are already clear and require only
brief summary. From the Jews outside of Palestine, obedience to neither the laws of
tithing nor the laws of ritual purity nor the agricultural taboos would be required. For the
Pharisees among them the conditions of life in exile were made considerably easier. But
this was done by effectively destroying the form of their earlier piety. We have no
evidence of what, if anything, was offered in its stead.

For Pharisees in Palestine the application of the primarily sectarian laws was to be
done in a more lenient way than earlier. Giving Heave-offering was simplified. One no
longer would have to distinguish between clean and unclean produce of the same species in
the same state but might give from the one for the other. Presumably other distinctions
formerly operative in the giving of Heave-offering would likewise be obscured. The laws
of the Seventh Year similarly would be applied less rigidly than earlier, if the case of the
hide anointed by Seventh-Year oil signifies a broader policy. Hence greater benefit from
the produce of the Seventh Year would be enjoyed by the pietists. It may be that the
more difficult conditions of economic life required some such lenient ruling, but we have
not a shred of evidence that economic considerations figured in Eliezer's enactments.

The Pharisaic custom of providing an 'eruv for carrying on the Sabbath was
extended, so that, first, a fence would be sufficient to establish a single courtyard,
however large; second, a person might simply buy a share in an 'eruv from a storekeeper;
third, for 'eruv-tavshilin any sort of food, not merely bread, might be used; and fourth,
dissenters or forgetful people would not be subject to pressure from their neighbors.

This last point suggests that Eliezer hoped to improve relationships between
Pharisees and other Jews, on the one side, and between Jews and Samaritans, on the
second. Eliezer allowed Jews to eat with Samaritans. Hence the xenophobia characteristic of the recent war was rejected in favor of a more irenic approach to relationships
within the Jewish community, formerly characterized by heated sectarian and civil strife,
and between Jewry and its neighbors, earlier marked by Jewish hostility toward closely
kindred groups.

The Sabbath rules were set aside in favor of other, equally important religious
duties. The tendency to erect ever higher walls around the Sabbath was thus countered by
Eliezer's view that the Sabbath was to be no more important than other religious
requirements. Its sanctity was separate and distinct from, and no greater than, that of
the coincident festival. Eliezer may have planned also to liberalize the rules governing
work on the intermediate days of a festival.

Vows were to be virtually excluded from the pious life. To be sure, temperamental people would continue to make them. But Eliezer would render the nullification of a vow a routine and simple matter. One might, on any pretext whatever, simply express regret that he had vowed, and the matter was done with. The dedication of one's property to the Temple -- which now would mean its destruction -- was limited. An oath to give the whole of one's property to the sanctuary was null. Presumably anyone in sufficient command of his senses to refrain from giving the whole lot would be unlikely to make such a gift to begin with. Likewise, a Nazir, subject to his earlier vow, would not be forced by last minute accidents into a perpetual renewal of the binding rules. His liability was limited to a few days, rather than to the repetition of the whole spell of Naziriteship.

Consistent with his leniency in the giving of tithes and Heave-offerings, Eliezer may have intended to limit the effect of the uncleanness rules by ruling that uncleanness pertains to no liquids, except, presumably, those specified in Scriptures. Here matters are less certain; we have a number of conflicting details which seem not wholly in accord with one another or with this basic principle. Certainly Eliezer wanted to make it easy to neutralize the prohibiting effects of holy materials which have fallen into secular produce or of impaired materials of the cult mixed with acceptable materials. The rules of neutralizing Heave-offering which has fallen into secular produce are enforced in a lenient way. Mixtures of bowls of blood or of blemished and unblemished sacrificial parts will be readily rendered fit for use on the pretext that one may easily remove the prohibited substance.

Eliezer's rules on the rights of women are at variance with these lenient tendencies. He seems to have consistently applied laws to the disadvantage of females, young and mature. A minor had no legal rights of protection. A woman might be divorced and yet not wholly free to remarry anyone she wanted. A woman was not to participate in the study of the law. Her husband theoretically might impose upon her the Sotah-rite for the slightest pretext or none at all. Eliezer's reforms stopped short of improving the situation of women, who, like the diasporan Jews, were given no important role in Pharisaic piety.

Eliezer evidently proposed for the cult to be ruled in accord with an orderly logic, which would settle all manner of details. What may have seemed to him illogical or inconsistent was to be rationalized. I do not see what practical consequences for the Yavnean situation were to be anticipated. Eliezer continued the earlier Pharisaic tendency to apply to the Parah-ceremony a less strict rule as to purity and other questions than was regarded by the Sadducees as proper. But this is not original to him and therefore has nothing to do with his Yavnean program.

One ethical issue seems important. Eliezer held that, faced with a choice of taking affirmative to prevent a possible violation of the law or of doing nothing at all, a person should assume responsibility and therefore take action. It would not be proper to disclaim responsibility and to stand aside. The contrary view was that one needs do nothing at all, so long as his own hands are not sullied.

In general, therefore, the tendency of Eliezer's own rulings seems to have been in a single direction, and that was toward the rationalization and the liberalization of the application of Pharisaic law. We cannot, to be sure, take for granted that all or even the very best attested traditions derive from Eliezer and have been formulated in his exact language. Nor is our interpretation of each detail necessarily the only possible way of seeing things. But if this view of Eliezer's own contribution is in the main valid, then it follows that what is asserted by the later tradition is absolutely correct: Eliezer really said nothing he had not heard from his masters. In an exact sense he was profoundly conservative. By attempting to reform details and to ease the strictness of the law, he hoped to conserve the Pharisaic way of piety substantially unchanged and unimpaired, essentially intact. This must mean that for Eliezer the destruction of the Temple did not mark a significant turning in the history of Judaism. Just as the destruction of the first Temple was followed, in a brief period, by the construction of the second, so he certainly supposed the same would now happen. He would see to it that the third Temple would be different from the second only in the more logical way in which its cult would be carried on, on the one side, and in the slightly simpler requirements of the application of the cult's purity rules to daily life and of the enforcement of the priestly taxes, on the other.

viii. Eliezer and the Christians

The comparison of Eliezer's legal agendum with that of the Synoptic Gospels will show a number of points at which Eliezer and the Christians were concerned with the same problems. In some of these both posited the same policy; in others they followed the same tendency; at still others they were diametrically opposed. The differences show what is already obvious: that the Christians knew and rejected Pharisaic piety, while Eliezer accepted and advocated it. Since the Synoptic picture reveals the situation prevailing after 70 -- whether or not its portrait likewise conforms to conditions before that time is not our problem -- we may make use of materials from all legal traditions attributed to Eliezer, in the theory that the Synoptics supply attestation for the issue contained in those traditions, if not for Eliezer's exact opinion on it.

1. Christian fasting: Pharisees and disciples of John fast, but Jesus's disciples do not -- Matt. 9:14-17 (Lk. 5:33-39, Mk. 2:18-22)
2. Picking grain on the Sabbath -- Matt. 12:1-8 (Lk. 6:1-5, Mk. 2:23-28)

1. No equivalent. The question does not occur in Eliezer's sayings, and he has no rulings on fasting, except in connection with rain.
2. No equivalent. Nor is the issue of healing on the Sabbath raised. But Jesus's stress that the sacrifices are done on the Sabbath is taken for granted in Eliezer's case of permitting the Passover and all its appurtenances to be carried out on the Sabbath, also circumcision. Eliezer's principle that the Sabbath is set aside by other religious considerations is consistent with the view attributed to Jesus that the Sabbath is no more important than other religious considerations -- in this case, the presence of the son of man.

3. You have heard... you shall not swear falsely, but shall perform to the Lord what you have sworn. But I say to you Do not swear at all, either by heaven... or by earth... or by Jerusalem... or by your hear -- Matt. 5:33-7.

3. Eliezer's view of swearing is different in form, but not much different in substance. He does not say one should not swear. But he says if one does, the oath is easily rendered of no effect.

4. Do not say, What shall we eat... Your heavenly father knows that you need them all -- Matt. 6:25-33 (Lk. 12:22-23).

4. The identical viewpoint is in b. Sot. 48b: One who worries about what he will eat on the morrow is among those of small faith.

5. A disciple is not above his teacher, but everyone when he is fully taught will be like his teacher -- Lk. 6:40 (Matt. 10:24-5).

5. Eliezer is said to have taught nothing but what he learned from his teacher. The (probably earlier) stories about his remaining silent when asked what he had not heard (or did not wish to tell) may be still more pertinent.

6. You say, If any one tells his father or his mother, What you have gained from me is given to God, he need not honor his father.
So for the sake of your tradition you have made void the word of God -- Matt. 15:1-6 (Mk. 7:9-13; Lk. 11:37-41).

6. This is a point of directly pertinent comparison, for Eliezer holds the same view in respect to the annulling of vows. He regards the honor of parents as sufficient grounds for releasing a man from his vow. Therefore one cannot deprive the father of his honor by means of a vow. Mk. is still more pointed: "If a man tells his father or mother, what you have gained from me is Corban..."

7. Not what goes into the mouth defiles a man, but what comes out of the mouth, this defiles a man -- Matt. 15:10-12 (Mk. 7:14ff).

7. This has no equivalent in Eliezer's sayings. He would have disagreed with the first statement, not necessarily with the second.

8. Scribes and Pharisees tithe mint and dill and cummin and neglect weightier matters of the law -- Matt. 23:23 (Lk. 11:42: mint and rue). but dill is merely illustrative, not significant in itself.

8. M. Ma. 4:5: Dill's seed, plant and pods are tithed, so Eliezer. Eliezer therefore will differ in respect to the exact detail.

9. Scribes and Pharisees cleanse the outside of the cup and of the plate -- Matt. 23:25 (Lk. 11:39; Mk. 7:3-4).

9. M. Toh. 8:7: The outer parts of vessels made unclean by liquids make the liquids unclean but do not make food invalid, so Eliezer. Joshua says they do. Simeon says liquids made unclean by the outer parts of vessels make other things unclean, etc. Accordingly, Jesus's saying that the outer parts of the cup and plate may convey uncleanness is in general congruent to the opinions of all three Yavneans, who hold that the outer parts can convey uncleanness, therefore have to be cleaned (purified).

10. Pharisees fast twice a week and give tithes of all that they get -- Lk. 18:12

10. The first point is without parallel, but the second certainly is to be taken for granted. To be sure it is not unique to Eliezer.

Eliezer's general tendency, which was in some details to ease the discipline of Pharisaic law, furthermore corresponds in a superficial way to the allegation that Jesus's burden is easy, while that of the Pharisees is difficult. But the issue seems to me external to the traditions about Eliezer, and for the Christians, what eased the Pharisaic discipline was its abrogation, not its lenient application.

The most striking points of contact are Nos. 2, 3, 4, 6, 8, and 9. The principle of Eliezer on the Sabbath's being set aside by the sacrifices is the same as the presupposition underlying Jesus's argument. It does not begin with either authority, to be sure. But they have in common the opinion that the Sabbath is no more important than various other commandments, and this is by no means clear to Eliezer's opposition. A second, and even more important point in common is the view that vowing is not to be encouraged. Jesus's instruction is not to vow at all. Eliezer's is to make vows of no effect. Both agree that a sign of faith is lack of anxiety about material things; Eliezer (like Yohanan b. Zakkai, b. Ber. 28b) would substitute anxiety about death, Jesus, about the coming of the kingdom. No. 6 is a more concrete illustration of the general idea of No. 3. Eliezer's revision of the law of vowing takes account of the sort of critique attributed to Jesus and vitiates its force by changing the rules of vowing so that one simply cannot in that way make void the word of God. The tithing of dill is important specifically to Eliezer; here is a point of contact and opposition. The same is so for cleansing the outsides of vessels, No. 9, but the tradition cannot begin with Eliezer. So on those points important to the Pharisaic discipline -- Nos. 7, 8, 9, 10 -- the two authorities will take opposite positions, for Eliezer was a Pharisee, and Jesus was not. But the two are in accord in respect to the 'philosophy' of the Sabbath (No. 2), vowing (Nos. 3, 6), faith (No. 4), and discipleship (No. 5). The Sabbath and vowing, moreover, represent important innovations on Eliezer's part and are central to Jesus' critique of the Pharisees; his third point, about a conflict between ritual and ethics, of course cannot have been taken seriously by people who saw no contradiction between the two.

One cannot derive from these facts the conclusion either that Eliezer was sympathetic to Christian viewpoints or that he was aware of, and opposed to, Christian criticism of Pharisaism. It seems, as to the former, that he too recognized anomalies perceived by the Christian Jews responsible for the pericopae in which those anomalies are important. The perpetual priority of the Sabbath certainly seemed to him dubious; the disruptive effects of vows for family life cannot have been unfamiliar, and his ruling is to be seen as an effort to counter a pernicious phenomenon. As to the latter, Eliezer took for granted the importance of tithing in general, and his ruling on dill represents nothing more than the application of well-established principles to trivial matter. All authorities in M. Toh. 8:7 take for granted that ritual uncleanness pertains to the outer sides of vessels; the point is not moot. But no one is entirely sure what effects follow from that fact -- and Jesus certainly is not clear on the point -- so the issue may be new to the Yavnean Pharisees or an old tradition may have required more careful definition. So the two striking points of conflict -- dill and the outer sides of vessels -- seem to represent matters of some, though modest, importance in the Yavnean period. Both points of noteworthy agreement -- Sabbath and vowing -- reveal Eliezer as unique among the early masters of Yavneh. While the view of the subordinated position of the Sabbath is attributed also to Hillel, the stories about Hillel and the Passover on the Sabbath first surface at Usha, while Eliezer's principle for circumcision on the Sabbath is well-attested at Yavneh and cannot be regarded as something he learned through the House of Hillel.

In this connection we may reconsider the allegation of W.D. Davies, The Setting of the Sermon on the Mount (Cambridge, 1964), p. 315:

> ... one fruitful way of dealing with the SM [Sermon on the Mount] is to regard it as the Christian answer to Jamnia [Yavneh]. Using terms very loosely, the SM is a kind of Christian, mishnaic counterpart to the formulation taking place there... It was the desire and necessity to present a formulation of the way of the New Israel at a time when the rabbis were engaged in a parallel task for the Old Israel that provided the outside stimulus for the Evangelist to shape the SM...

The striking points of contact between Eliezer's legal agendum and that of the Synoptic Gospels -- which center, as is to be expected, on the Pharisaic pericopae and therefore on Matt. 23/Matt. 7 and parallels -- support Davies' interpretation. Naturally, the Synoptic view of Jesus focuses upon the Temple period and its issues. The Synoptics' Pharisaism is the pre-70 Pharisaism of tithing, ritual purity, and related matters. Their critique is that these are not so important as ethical actions. The points of congruence with Eliezer underline the larger similarity, for he too is a figure out of pre-70 Pharisaism, rather than of scribism or post-70 rabbinism.

Jesus is portrayed not only as an anti-Pharisee, but also as a kind of scribe-rabbi, who teaches the Torah of Moses and is an authoritative interpreter of Scriptures -- a role in which the Synoptic writers never cast a Pharisee. The Synoptics' Pharisees are not represented as teachers of Torah or preachers in synagogues or lawyers in charge of the application of law or the administration of justice. Those sorts of scribes or "rabbis" also exhibit important activities in common with Jesus. Accordingly, the Synoptics' Jesus stands in close relationship both with Pharisees and with scribes. He is opposed to the piety of the one and stands against the authority of the other. But his teachings in important ways take for their detailed agenda the legal issues and problems of Pharisaism -- and not all of these are resolved in a negative way -- and he stands very close indeed to the conceptual world of Pharisaism. And his activities evidently were seen as the sorts of things a scribe, at least of the lower class, would have done. In a general way, therefore, the Synoptics' Jesus constitutes an amalgam of the formerly separate and distinctive traits of Pharisaism and scribism -- a peculiarly Yavnean phenomenon.

CHAPTER SIX

THE ELIEZER OF TRADITION

i. Introduction

The Eliezer of tradition emerges from pericopae which cannot be shown to have been redacted either close to Eliezer's own times or among his disciples and contemporaries or their direct successors. But the themes and often the principles and detailed opinions of those pericopae are closely related to materials deriving from authorities who, for various reasons, ought to have known what they were talking about. The materials before us are called traditions because they represent either a later state in the evolution of historically valuable pericopae or an addition to those pericopae which may well have begun in the earlier stages of the formation of Eliezer's materials. We certainly do not suppose that materials unattested by Yavneans or Ushans cannot have been known in Yavnean or Ushan times. We maintain only that such materials cannot be regarded as of the same order of reliability. When, however, we know for sure that themes, principles, or even detailed opinions in unattested pericopae first occurring in Mishnah-Tosefta relate closely to what has already been attested in earlier strata, we may claim sound reason to introduce such pericopae into an account of the historical Eliezer. In regard to numerous pericopae the new materials have been developed on the basis of established ones; and in regard to others new materials are consistent in theme with the already attested agenda.

ii. Topics of the Law

1. Agricultural Rules, Tithes, and Taboos

Land in which one may sow a quarter-qav of seed -- ten and a fifth amot square -- is liable for the Pe'ah-gift. Aqiba says a much smaller plot is liable. A vineyard wholly made up of defective clusters belong to its owner. Aqiba says it belongs to the poor. Both rulings on Eliezer's part favor the landowner. One who keeps thorns in a vineyard forfeits the adjacent vines. Since the man has kept the thorns, it is assumed he wants them. They therefore are of value, and the taboo against mixed seeds will apply.

Arum which has grown in the Seventh Year belongs to the poor. Joshua says the poor have no claim on it. Eliezer's view is that the poor alone may eat after the beginning of the Seventh Year taboo. If one has three kinds of vegetables pickled in a single jar, as soon as one of them becomes prohibited by reason of the advent of the Seventh Year, the others may not be used either. Joshua says the opposite, and Gamaliel says one goes by the species, and their being pickled together is of no account. If one receives Seventh Year fruits as a gift or inheritance, he has to give them to people who eat Seventh Year produce. The sages say they are to be sold, not given away, and the money is then to be divided among everyone. The difference is that the sages do not want to reward the sinner. Eliezer will regard the money as prohibited, just like the fruit; the sages say it is in effect to be left ownerless.

If a person wants to give more than the required minimum of Heave-offering, he may give as much as a tenth of the crop. Ishmael says he may give as much as a half. Tarfon and Aqiba say he may give virtually the whole crop. If a se'ah of unclean Heave-offering fell into a hundred of clean unconsecrated food, one may raise up that unclean se'ah, for the one which fell in is raised up, then burned. The sages say one needs to do nothing, for the unclean se'ah is neutralized and may be consumed. If a hundred of unclean Heave-offering fell into a hundred of clean Heave-offering, it is taken up and burned. The sages say it is neutralized. If a se'ah of Heave-offering fell into a hundred of unconsecrated food, and a new se'ah has been raised up and then has fallen elsewhere, Eliezer rules it is treated like certain Heave-offering, and the sages say it is not, unless it is in the prescribed proportion. If a se'ah of Heave-offering fell into less than a hundred of unconsecrated food, and the whole was then subjected to the law of Heave-offering, and some of the mixture fell elsewhere, Eliezer holds the new mixture is regarded as certain Heave-offering, and sages say it is not, except in prescribed proportion. If a person by mistake ate Heave-offering, he has to repay its value and an added fifth. Eliezer says he may pay back from one kind instead of from another, consistent with his opinion that one may give from clean for unclean produce. Aqiba says one pays back the same kind.

If a person takes clean olives from the press, he is liable to tithes when he nibbles on them. But if they are unclean, he is not liable. Salting them acts as the completion of their processing, so they are liable to tithes. But if they are possibly going to be returned to the vat, they are not finished. One tithes dill, caperbush, and mustard. He who separates Second Tithe is presumed to have separated the First. The sages say the opposite is the case. If a man has given the principle of the Second Tithe but not the added Fifth, he may eat the produce; the sages say he may not. Judah the Patriarch agrees with Eliezer for the Sabbath, but not for the weekday. After the destruction of the Temple, Eliezer was told that he had to continue to bring up the produce and redeem it in, or near, Jerusalem (but that law is not attributed to Eliezer in Tos., and in b. Bes. 5a/b. R.H. 31b it is explicitly attributed to Yohanan b. Zakkai).

Produce from Palestine which is taken abroad is liable for Dough-offering, for it was obligated as soon as it was prepared. Aqiba holds that the person is not liable when abroad. Small bits of dough adhere together to form the quantity liable for the Dough-offering.

Israelites who are sharecroppers for gentiles in Syria must give Tithes and are liable to observe the Seventh Year. Syria is therefore regarded by Eliezer as Jewish property, no different from Palestine. Gamaliel differs.

One may not curdle milk with the sap of 'orlah-fruit. Joshua says one may do so with the sap of leaves and roots, but not of unripe figs, and all take for granted one may not use the fruit (as the Scripture makes clear). If leaven of unconsecrated food and of Heave-offering have fallen into dough, but in each was an insufficient quantity to leaven dough, while together they do so, Eliezer says the part that completed the quantity sufficient to leaven the dough will be decisive. If it is the Heave-offering, the whole is prohibited; otherwise the whole is permitted. The sages say it does not matter; the prohibited species only is taken into account if by itself it can produce the leavening. If one has anointed dishes with unclean oil and then done so with clean, or vice versa, Eliezer says one decides whether the vessel is clean or unclean by which oil was applied first. The sages say one decides according to which was applied last. Eliezer says one should use the unclean oil first, then the clean.

2. Sabbaths and Festivals

One may put bread into the oven at dusk on the Sabbath if there is time for the bottom surface to form a crust. It is permissible to carry a sword, spear, or club on the Sabbath, for these are adornments. A wick of cloth which has been twisted but not singed is not used for the Sabbath-lamp; it is necessary by an actual deed to demonstrate its purpose as a wick for the lamp, not merely by twisting. A woman may wear a tiara on the Sabbath; it is regarded as an ornament. On the Sabbath one may not write on his flesh by scratching. One may not weave three threads at the beginning of a web or one onto what is woven. If a window-shutter is not fastened to the window-frame it may not be used to close the window on the Sabbath. Similarly, one is not to spread a cloak over a Sukkah. But he may stretch out the filter on the festival day and may on the Sabbath pour wine through a filter which is already stretched out. In order to render an alley-way valid, one must erect two side-posts.

Passover overrides the Sabbath in all respects -- a point consistent with Eliezer's view of circumcision on the Sabbath. A person is exempt from keeping the first Passover if he is on a distant journey, which is anywhere beyond the threshold of the Temple court (an opinion attested by Yosi).

If the goat used for the Atonement rite fell ill, it is not to be carried. If the one who is to send him forth fell ill, another is not appointed in his place. If the goat was pushed down the hill and did not die, the agent is not to go down and kill it. Thus if the rite cannot be carried out under normal circumstances, it is not to be fulfilled by extraordinary means.

On the festival a disciple is to stay home with his family.

If an animal and its offspring fell into the pit on the festival, one may raise the first on condition of slaughtering it for use on the festival, and one slaughters it, but leaves the first in the pit and feeds it there.

If the community fasted and rain fell before noon, the fast is not to be completed. Others say only if the rains came before dawn is the fast cancelled.

In respect to the rules of mourning, Asseret [Pentecost] is regarded as the Sabbath, Gamaliel says the New Year and Day of Atonement are treated as festivals. According to Eliezer, Asseret counts in the required seven and thirty days of mourning, but does not interrupt the count; it is added to the total.

3. Family Affairs

A eunuch sterilized by exposure to the sun submits to halisah, and his brothers do so with his wife, because he may be healed. But one made so by man may not, since he can never have a remedy for his condition. Eliezer's interpretation of the old tradition, which held that a eunuch both does and does not submit to halisah, competes with Aqiba's, who interprets matters contrariwise. Halisah is not to be done at night. It may be done with the left foot. If the woman drew off the shoe and pronounced the required formula but did not actually spit, the act is invalid. If two sisters who were deaf-mutes, one of age and the other a minor, married brothers, and the husband of the minor died, his wife is exempt from Levirate marriage by virtue of being 'the sister of his wife.' Eliezer says that if the husband of the adult wife died, the minor is instructed to exercise the right of refusal against him. Gamaliel says it is better if she comes of age, and then the other will be exempt as the sister of his wife. Joshua takes a still more stringent position. Once a woman is permitted to the Levir, if he then dies, she may marry anyone at all. That is, once free of the Levirate connection, a woman permanently remains so.

A woman may marry on the evidence of a single witness that her former husband has died.

A woman's claims as to the cause of her sexual status are to be accepted. Thus if a woman says that after her betrothal she was raped and therefore has not lost her rights, she is to be believed.

A woman past puberty, or one who has waited twelve months after betrothal, or a widow thirty days from when the betrother has sought to complete the marriage may rely upon her prospective husband to annul her vows. One who awaits Levirate marriage may have her vows annulled by her prospective brother-in-law even where there is more than one Levir. Vows may be annulled in advance by a husband for his wife -- that is, even before they have been made. In all three rulings, Eliezer continues the policy of rendering vows of no account.

One should not teach Torah to his daughter.

The most casual testimony is sufficient to warrant a man's divorcing his wife and paying her Ketuvah, if he has already warned her not to 'go aside in secret,' that is, not to commit adultery.

Four types of women may rely on their normal period in determining whether they are unclean by reason of the menstrual period: the virgin, the pregnant woman, the nursing mother, and the old woman. Joshua says he heard only the virgin may do so. The dispute of Eliezer and Joshua deals with a point at issue between Shammai and Hillel, but while the language of Eliezer is the same as the formulation given to Shammai, the opinion is different. Shammai says all women may do so, and Hillel says all women have to rely upon their examination. Yosi then differs from both, specifying only the pregnant woman and the nursing mother who have missed three periods. The attestation derives from Judah the Patriarch, who is said to have ruled according to Eliezer. M. states that the law follows Eliezer. Tos. supplies: "In Eliezer's lifetime, people would follow his opinion, but after he died, Joshua restored matters to their former condition" -- meaning, to his version of the law. y. has just the opposite. Presumably because M. claims Eliezer's opinion is normative, y. has reversed the situation with Joshua.

There is no way for a mamzer to purify himself from his mamzerut.

4. Theoretical Problems

A high priest must make himself unclean with a neglected corpse, if the only alternative is a Nazir's doing so. If a Nazir suddenly contracts uncleanness during the final sacrifice, he loses those sacrifices which have already been made. The whole thing is to be done over again, because the sacrifices must be offered all together.

If a neglected corpse is found exactly between two cities, both cities bring heifers. If the head is found in one place and the body in another, the head is brought to the body. For measuring the location of the neglected corpse, one begins from the navel.

5-6. Theory of the Cult. The Temple and Sacrifice

A Sin-offering and a Guilt-offering are subject to the same rules, because both are brought in expiation of sins. The Whole-offering of a bird offered below the red line after the manner of the Sin-offering and for the sake of the sin-offering is subject to the law of sacrilege -- an opinion based on a logical argument.

The substitute of a Guilt-offering is treated like the substitute of a Sin-offering. The progeny of a terefah may not be offered on the altar. A firstling may be redeemed with a hybrid, but not with a koy. If one deliberately rendered a firstling unfit by slitting its ear, it may never be slaughtered, even though some other blemish may later occur in it.

The means of man's livelihood -- his ox or his tools -- may not be taken as a pledge for the vow of Valuation. This is consistent with the rule that one may not give to the Temple his whole property.

A heifer whose neck is broken should be in her first year, and the Red Heifer should be two years old. A Red Heifer for the Sin-offering rite that was pregnant is valid. It may not be purchased from gentiles. It may be born of Caesarean section or may be purchased with the hire of a harlot or the price of a dog. It may have as many as fifty scattered black or white hairs. It is not subject to ordinary Temple rules. Therefore one does not require the appropriate intention. It may be slaughtered by a priest with unwashed hands and feet. Intention in no respect will render invalid the Red-Heifer sacrifice. A reed pipe cut freshly from the ground for holding the water or ashes of the Sin-offering should be immersed immediately. Whatever is susceptible to become unclean on account of corpse-uncleanness, whether unclean or clean, is not regarded with respect to one occupied with the Sin-offering water as unclean with maddaf-uncleanness. If a jar containing the ashes of the Sin-offering is placed on top of a dead creeping thing, it remains clean. One clean for the Sin-offering rite who moved a creeping thing is regarded as still clean. Loosely-fastened boards are unclean in what concerns Sin-offering water. If one has been sprinkled by means of hyssop-berries, he is regarded as clean in respect to coming to the sanctuary.

7. Sources of Uncleanness

An olive's bulk of worm from a corpse, whether alive or dead, is unclean, like the corpse's actual flesh. The ash of a cremated corpse renders unclean if it is a quarter-qav in quantity, just like a bone. A grave-stone renders unclean by carrying. A tomb which is equal, top and bottom, renders unclean him who touches it on any spot. If there was a projection on a projecting window above the window, and uncleanness is under the projection, it does not bring uncleanness into the house. A grave-area may make a grave-area.

The semen of a Zab does not render something susceptible to uncleanness as a liquid. Whatever is carried on carrion is unclean. One who carries the flux of a Zab is unclean.

8. Persons Subject to Ritual Uncleanness

He who eats food unclean at a first-grade uncleanness is regarded as unclean at a first level of uncleanness, and so with second and third.

If a woman was in hard labor for three days out of eleven and had relief from her pains for twenty-four hours and then gave birth, she is regarded as a Zabah. If she had hard labor during the eighty days of purifying of the female child, all the blood she sees until the abortion comes out is unclean.

9. Objects Subject to Ritual Uncleanness

The comb-shaped filter of the water cooler is unsusceptible of receiving uncleanness. If a small coin can drop through a hole in a lamp, the lamp is no longer susceptible of uncleanness. An oven cut up into rings is regarded as broken, and even though it is then reconstructed with sand between each ring, it is still broken and therefore clean. If a bucket, a boiler, a cauldron, a jug, or a wine- or oil-measure is broken so that it can no longer hold a small coin, it is capable of becoming unclean. A baker's shelf fixed to a wall is clean. A wooden vessel becomes clean if the objects usually kept in it can drop through a hole which has been made in it. A patch of new cloth which is thrown out is rendered unsusceptible to uncleanness.

A quarter-log of drawn water at the outset invalidates the ritual pool. If a person has left wine-jars on the roof to dry out, and they were filled with rain-water, during the rainy season they may be broken into the cistern which contains a little water. But if there is no water in the cistern, they may not be broken. If a plasterer forgot his lime-pot in the cistern, and it was filled with water, if the water of the pool floated over it in any amount, it may be broken, so that its water may replenish the pool. But if not, it may not be broken. One may immerse himself in the water of an immersion pool which has in it water and mud, but not in the mud of such a pool.

10. The Courts

Wild animals do not have to be tried. They may be killed at random. But an ox which has killed a man is tried by a court of twenty-three judges.

12. The Age

On that day the sages overfilled the measure, -- that is, the Shammaites' decrees were excessive.

The destruction of the Temple marked the decline in the generations. Sages became like scribes. No one now seeks (wisdom). One can rely only on God.

While excommunicated, Eliezer approved a decision of the assembly of sages that Ammon and Moab give Poorman's Tithe in the Seventh Year, attributing it to Yohanan and thence to Moses.

Eliezer was arrested on suspicion of being a min.

Gentiles have no portion of the world to come.

13. New Subjects

One reads the Shema' in the evening until the end of the first watch. In the morning, one may do so from the time that it is possible to distinguish between blue and green. One should not follow a fixed text in prayer but should make up something new every day. This rule produces the further observation that there are times that a brief prayer is called for, and times that one should pray at length. The havdalah-prayer, "Favors man with knowledge," should be inserted in the Thanksgiving-blessing and not be said as a blessing by itself. Evidently Eliezer qualified his rule about not having a fixed liturgy; this would apply to the supplications but not to the introductory and concluding blessings of the Eighteen Benedictions. Or he contradicts himself with respect to the havdalah.

One is prohibited from doing a magical deed but is permitted to create the illusion of having done a magical deed.

If a man kindles a fire in his own property, it may spread sixteen cubits in every direction for him to be accountable for the damages it causes.

It is forbidden to raise dogs in Palestine.

Merely walking in a property constitutes an act of acquisition. One may make a verbal will, whether healthy or dying; real estate is thereby to be acquired by money, writ, or usucaption, and movables are acquired only by usucaption -- thus a verbal will in and of itself will not be of effect. But the real issue before Eliezer should be whether there is a distinction between acquiring real estate and movables, and he says there is. Then "walking" is insufficient for real estate, so Eliezer has contradictory opinions.

If one slaughters a dying animal and the blood spurts forth, it is valid slaughtering; the animal need not jerk a leg. A cock-partridge is functionally the same as the dam, and therefore one may not take both the partridge and the eggs.

Eliezer has a good memory.

Eliezer said one should be as concerned for his fellow's honor as he is for his own, should be patient, should repent a day before dying, and should not get too close to the sages.

iii. Origins, Early Life, Education

While the Eliezer of tradition is given little more of a biography than the Eliezer of history, two important biographical themes first occur in the materials before us. To be sure, no one alludes to his station in life or to his beginnings as an ignorant man. But the relationship to Yohanan is made explicit in M. Avot and is central in M. Yad. Furthermore, some sort of excommunication is alluded to in M. Yad. A story about Eliezer's excommunication therefore ought to have circulated before ca. 250 A.D It may be that the reference to the "oven of 'Akhnai" in M. Kel. 5:1 is not a later gloss, in which case the introductory element of the story of the excommunication was already settled. But the details of the story are hardly attested in this stratum of traditions.

The relationship to Yohanan is another matter. Yohanan originally is presented as praising Eliezer: "If all the sages in Israel were in one scale of the balance, and Eliezer ben Hyrcanus in the other, he would outweigh them all." That this saying is primary to the primitive structure of the pericope is proven by the list of disciples in M. Avot 2:9, which places Eliezer at the head of the list. It is further demonstrated by Abba Saul's correction of Yohanan's saying, which explicitly alludes to the primary form and rejects it: "If all the sages of Israel were in one scale... and Eliezer with them, and Eliezer b. 'Arakh were in the other, he would outweigh them all." If Abba Saul's saying is authentic, then he would supply an important attestation both to the original list and to the tradition of Eliezer's discipleship with Yohanan. In that case, the tradition goes back to late Yavneh or early Usha. The purpose of the correction -- to replace Eliezer by Eliezer -- is served also by the Go forth-sayings, which reflect the original sequence of disciples, with Eliezer first, and then contradict it by turning the last saying into a climax, so that the first is made least and the last is made greatest. The same hand which inserted this may also have reversed the attributions of Eliezer and Eliezer, for it is better to be a flowing spring than a plastered cistern. (That it is better to come first than last is shown by the question, "Why did the House of Hillel merit having the law following their opinion? ...Because they were kindly and modest, and placed the opinion of the House of Shammai ahead of their own." So they gave the advantage to the opposition -- a sign of modesty.)

It seems that the downgrading of Eliezer, which breaks the symmetry of the form, reflects the (still mysterious) event involving his disgrace and excommunication. The sayings which put him first ought to antedate these events. But if they do, they establish what no internal evidence even hints at, namely the discipleship with Yohanan. They possibly come from Eliezer's own circle and probably would have surprised Yohanan himself. At any rate we have no reason to suppose the highly stylized materials in M. Avot 2:8-9 derive from Yohanan himself.

M. Yad. 4:3 is firm on Eliezer's having studied with Yohanan. It is an equally peculiar pericope. It represents Eliezer as living in isolation from the other masters, though it does not explain why. Still, the story is further evidence that something has happened to set Eliezer apart, though the details have not yet been made definite. Yosi the son of Damascene is then asked, "What new thing came up in the house of study today" -- the first indication that the Yavnean gathering constituted a "house of study." Yosi then tells Eliezer that the group has voted that Ammon and Moab give Poorman's Tithe in the Seventh Year. Eliezer says that is exactly what he heard from Yohanan. The original debate involves Tarfon, who says they must give Poorman's Tithe, and Eliezer b. ^CAzariah, who assigns them Second Tithe, with Joshua and Ishmael siding with Tarfon. Gamaliel is not included in the pericope, but he does appear in M. Yad. 4:4. And in M. Yad. 4:2, Eliezer himself occurs, to be sure, in an interpolation irrelevant to the pericope. The larger setting therefore is puzzling.

Still more curious is the representation of the whole assembly as imposing on the lands of Ammon and Moab the Jewish agricultural taxes. Yohanan is now discovered to have been a crypto-revolutionary -- not alone, but along with the whole of the on-that-day consistory, which now includes, in redactional context, both Eliezer (explicitly) and Gamaliel (implicitly)! The inclusion of Eliezer is not impossible, for M. 4:3 forthwith excludes him; Gamaliel can be accounted for in the theory that he participated as a private person, no longer as nasi.

But the content of the saying attributed to Yohanan via Eliezer is as suspicious as its form; both are probably fraudulent. The secret teaching was revealed by Eliezer only when he was in a state of excommunication, so that he never is given the opportunity to deny the reported revelation at the actual consistory. The story is incredible. But the problem of who made it up cannot be neglected (see below, section v, p. 110).

The materials before us therefore lead to the supposition that Eliezer was a disciple of Yohanan. His early life is still unilluminated. But no one now doubts Eliezer was a student of Torah and derived his traditions from the first master of Yavneh. The traditions moreover underline the already-evident motif that something has happened to isolate Eliezer from his colleagues but are not clear on exactly what might have happened. It is taken for granted, however, that he was by himself. Had he been excommunicated, Yosi should not have had to come to him -- later stories say even Aqiba kept his distance -- so perhaps the excommunication was not yet part of the account of Eliezer's "estrangement." But we have no better idea of what might have been alleged.

iv. Eliezer's Active Career

We have no evidence about what Eliezer actually did either for a living or within the Yavnean gathering. To be sure, the problem of what to do with fruits of the Second Tithe suggests he possessed some sort of land and farmed it. But we do not know how large were his possessions or how much of an income was yielded by them. The same source says they were at Lydda, and since most materials -- except the Aqiba-centered death-scene -- are firm on placing Eliezer there, we do not have to wonder where he lived. His reference in M. Git. 1:1 to Lydda further suggests, but does not confirm, that he spent time there.

This means he was not domiciled at Yavneh. Indeed, no available tradition places him in Yavneh at any point in his career, so we do not know his relationship to the gathering there. Perhaps a number of local authorities (but we do not know what their authority consisted of) were in communication with the Yavnean gathering or with Gamaliel himself but spent the bulk of their time in their own towns.

The story about the fast in Lydda further suggests that Eliezer exercised some sort of religious authority in the town; we do not know upon what basis or for what areas of ordinary life. The view that he was able to effect his view of what to do in connection with circumcision on the Sabbath reenforces the theory that in Lydda he was an authority in minor matters of religious practice. He is not represented as a civil administrator; he did not judge cases of torts, damages, or other domestic conflict; he had no place in the administration of justice, criminal (except for homicidal oxen) or otherwise.

To be sure, he would now seem to have had disciples in attendance, but we still do know for what purpose he gathered and educated them, nor are we certain he bestowed upon them any form of certification or rabbinical recognition. The stories about relationships to disciples concern festival behavior -- covering the Sukkah with a cloak, spending Sukkot at home, and domestic matters -- mourning practices and the like. He is further represented as being asked a series of questions about the Day of Atonement, and these questions, reenforced by the traditions in quite different form handed on in Eliezer's name by Judah, strongly suggest he taught laws about the Temple's rites on that day.

In all, therefore, we may safely suppose Eliezer did teach some laws, and, so far as the disciples' involvement is concerned, they were about festival behavior and Temple rites on the holy day -- not much of a legacy. The stories in M. Neg. 9:3 and 11:7 further portray him as explaining inherited traditions and approving the explanation of disciples. We need not doubt, therefore, that he held and handed on antecedent traditions of some sort; they need not have been limited to the cult and the sacred calendar. But it is difficult to demonstrate what other topics were included.

v. Eliezer's Historical Situation. Pharisaism and Rabbinism

The established view of Eliezer as a Pharisee certainly is confirmed by the topics and substance of the materials before us. He still has no "rabbinical" sayings about study of Torah and the like. Strikingly, he does say it is better to stay home on the festival than to come to the master. Later versions of the saying produce a sermon making the opposite point, now in accord with the rabbinical view about the priority of study of Torah, therefore of the master over the family. Perhaps the first instruction was thus revised to make Eliezer conform to later opinion on the subject. While a large number of sayings pertains to the Temple, none affirms that study of Torah is equivalent to sacrifice or that the rabbi is the new priest or similarly important rabbinical allegations.

What is strikingly new in the traditions is the claim that Eliezer was in favor of war in general and of the expansion of the Jews' territories in and around Palestine in particular. To be sure, the whole of the Yavnean consistory is represented as imposing upon Moab and Ammon the Jewish agricultural taxes, so in this respect Eliezer is supposed to have contributed the approval of Yohanan b. Zakkai, a remarkable and incredible claim. To that claim one must add Eliezer's own view that Syria is to be regarded as no different from Palestine. What this means is that the Jews are regarded by him as rightful owners of Syria, as much as of Palestine, and therefore must pay the same taxes they would pay if living within the borders of Jewish Palestine. To effect such a claim obviously would involve the Jews in a greater war than that of 66-73. Gamaliel is further represented as opposing Eliezer on this question, and well he might, for he was supposed to have been the Jews' delegate to the Roman government and could hardly have joined those who would foster a new war against Rome and extend the limits of the war to include the nearby diaspora communities. Eliezer's opinion on war -- expressed in the rule that a sword is an ornament -- is consistent. To these laws one may add the sentiment that gentiles have no portion in the world to come. The mamzer likewise may not improve his status -- so a generalized xenophobia, appropriate to the laws about the status of Syria and carrying a sword on the Sabbath, extended to the excluded caste of Israel itself.

These allegations, first occurring all at once in the stratum of traditions about Eliezer, do not necessarily contradict the quite contrary allegations of the historically reliable stratum composed of the best and better traditions. It may be argued that approving an alliance with the Samaritans was meant to correct a major error in the earlier war, for it was now clear that the Jews could do nothing without reliable allies. The liberalization of the Pharisaic discipline and the mitigation of its effects on non-Pharisees likewise might constitute an effort to unify the local population and to limit the decisive effects of the peculiar practices of what was now the regnant, or at least, a highly influential, sect. The declaration that the whole discipline would not apply to the diasporan communities would produce the same effect. In the event of Pharisaic domination of a reconstituted, and greatly enlarged, Jewish state, it would be unnecessary for the diasporan Jews to undertake the expensive tithes and the onerous unclean-ness-taboos of the Pharisees. Their Sabbath rule would, moreover, be imposed lightly. But, to be sure, this concession would not effect the immediately surrounding countries -- Syria, Moab, and Ammon -- which would be incorporated into the greater state. I see no connection, to be sure, between this proposed interpretation of the new materials and Eliezer's opinion that the generation of the wilderness will inherit the world to come; I cannot imagine any special group of Jews of the first century who traced their lineage back to that generation in particular.

It therefore seems possible to harmonize the portrait given by the best and better traditions with the sharply different one presented in the fair ones. But the two are so clearly at variance with one another, and each is so strikingly limited to its own stratum, that an alternative explanation may be called for. The historical Eliezer, like his alleged master, Yohanan, indeed did oppose war in general and (possibly) the war against Rome in particular; he did seek to alleviate the burden of the Pharisaic discipline on non-Pharisees and to limit its demands upon Pharisees and did propose a more tolerant attitude toward non-Jews in Palestine and Jews in the diaspora. Then the Eliezer of history is misre-presented in the stratum of traditions. He is now alleged to have advanced the opposite of his former policies. So the new materials come later and strikingly revise and contradict the old.

At what point in the evolution of the tradition would such a complete revision of his former attitudes have been introduced? It cannot have derived either from Aqiba or from Ilai, both of whom play important parts in the earliest portrait. Then it should have either come from a different set of Yavneans or, more likely, appeared after Yavneh, some time between ca. 120 and ca. 180. In that case the predominant party in the production of traditions will have been the disciples of Aqiba, who themselves probably favored the war of Bar Kokhba and therefore insisted their master, Aqiba, was among his supporters, and retroactively turned into militarists not only Eliezer, but also Yohanan himself, indeed along with the whole of the Yavnean consistory assembled, according to their claim, <u>on that day</u>. Then only Gamaliel is left out of the war-party. It would have been difficult to claim otherwise, with Gamaliel's son Simeon in charge of the Ushan authority and his grandson Judah in closest ties with the Roman regime itself. The revision of the historical Eliezer into an xenophobic militarist therefore does not stand alone in the treatment of the Yavnean materials. The disciples of Aqiba did far more to revolutionize the former picture of Yohanan (<u>Development of a Legend</u>, pp. 16-17, 27-29). Eliezer cannot be seen as a particularly important figure. What appears likely is that wherever they could invent stories to show Yavneans favored war against Rome, they did so. When it was possible to turn an uncompromising statement in favor of pacifism into an ambiguous statement that study of Torah would guarantee success, they also did so. These large tendencies touched -- if lightly -- upon the traditions about Eliezer and produced allegations strikingly at variance with the first, and more accurate picture. But this revision was not everywhere effected in the formulation of traditions about Eliezer and did not evidently produce the systematic effort to falsify existing allegations to the contrary.

The Eliezer of tradition therefore is represented in a way we could not have anticipated on the basis of the materials behind the Eliezer of history. The changes, though few, are discrete and unrelated and do not look as though they are the product of a single hand or a single circle. They therefore should be seen as representative of a larger tendency on the part of a considerable part of a generation of authorities to justify war and foster militarism and xenophobia. But the historical Eliezer ought to have had no part in such an approach to the Jews' relationships to other peoples in general and to Rome in particular. He had lived through the disastrous war and witnessed the destruction of the Temple. How he proposed to secure the right to rebuild the Temple and reconstitute its cult we do not know. He might, to be sure, have expected that war would serve to accomplish these messianic purposes. But having seen the inability of the Jews to unite in one war and their proved tendency to alienate the neighboring peoples, he ought to have sought another, more promising way toward the same end. That way can only have been collaboration with Rome, not sedition or rebellion.

Since Gamaliel, alleged to have been Eliezer's brother-in-law, almost certainly advanced exactly that policy, it is not far-fetched to claim that Eliezer did likewise. Among the masters of the Yavnean period, he ought to have taken the part of the patriarch. Among the opposition should have been both Aqiba and his close associate,

Joshua. Since both the deposition of Gamaliel and the excommunication of Eliezer are represented as the result of encounters with Joshua -- in the one case because of the patriarch's "high-handedness" and in the other because of Eliezer's failure to accede to the opinion of the "majority" -- it would appear that the war party was led by, or at least claimed to rely upon the authority of, Joshua and Aqiba. Now that claim in regard to Aqiba stands against the internal evidences already surveyed, which have Aqiba as a major authority for Eliezer's traditions overall and for the ones friendly to Samaritans and others in particular. If we rely upon the materials attested by Aqiba and Ilai, we have to reject those evidently produced by the Ushan successors of Aqiba. But then Aqiba's testimony with respect to Eliezer contradicts the later view of Aqiba himself. Similarly, the sayings attributed to Yohanan in favor of peace are contradicted by those appearing in documents attributed to Aqiba's disciples. So it is the disciples -- or authorities claiming to be disciples -- who have revised the pictures not only of Eliezer and Yohanan, but possibly of Aqiba himself. Of this, obviously, we cannot be certain.

vi. Eliezer's Own Contribution

While it is difficult to distinguish Eliezer's own innovations from his application to new problems or cases of established principles, it seems probable that a number of principles do originate with him, and he also participated with his colleagues in the solution of problems heretofore not resolved or even considered.

The liturgical issues probably begin with the early Yavneans. In this regard Eliezer's position is his own and contrary to that attributed to everyone else. He did not wish to standardize the supplicatory part of the Eighteen Benedictions and insisted that the former situation prevail. That is, he wished prayer to remain primarily an expression of the private person and not subject to the discipline of the law. Still, he accepted the need to define when the Shema' was to be said morning and night, so he evidently acceded to the tendency to standardize important elements of liturgy, preserving the individual's initiatives in those matters particularly pertinent to his own situation, particularly the supplications in the Prayer.

His view that the poor may use Seventh Year fruit is consistent with the principle of the House of Shammai. In several other cases involving Seventh Year fruit, he was consistently lenient. And this is an established trait of his laws.

His principle on the neutralization of mixtures of sacred substances, e.g., in the cult, or Heave-offering, surely begins with him. Likewise, the tradition has developed the view about giving Heave-offering from clean produce to its logical next step: One may pay back from one kind for another.

As observed, many laws constitute nothing more than the application to new, trivial matters of established rules, e.g., tithing was everywhere required, but Eliezer said dill, caperbush, and mustard had also to be tithed.

If Eliezer actually is responsible for the sayings about the liability of Syria and other neighboring countries to Palestinian agricultural taxes, then of course these sayings are originated by him. Likewise, his approval of war begins with him -- in context. But it was a commonplace opinion.

The view, already known, that the Sabbath is subordinate to other commandments -- circumcision, the Passover -- is new to Eliezer and a major innovation, extending the principle that the cult is carried on to other matters.

He likewise would evidently require everyone not in the Temple to keep the second, not the first, Passover. This means that after 70 everyone will have to keep Passover at the same time, and the (alleged) earlier practice will have been abrogated.

Most of the opinions on the problem of Levirate marriage and on accepting the testimony of a woman in explanation of her sexual status look new. The tradition has developed Eliezer's effort to make it easy to annul vows to some new matters, no more extreme than the original allegation.

It is difficult to claim that with Eliezer begins the view that acquiring real estate is done differently from acquiring movables. The distinction is old. But the pericope, according to our analysis, lays the claim that Eliezer said one requires the one to be done in a more elaborate way than the other. The issues and rules in respect to slaughter and the firstling look new but do not exhibit an important or fundamental attitude. The cases of Kelim and Ohalot, as stated, reveal nothing more than a tendency to apply old principles to new objects, in the one case, or to invent new problems for consideration according to established law, in the other.

The distinction between the Parah-rite and the normal Temple rite is represented as original to Eliezer, and so it may have been. But the same distinction is present in other materials attributed to early Yavneans. Eliezer's new distinctions in respect to the ritual pool, which tended to make the law more stringent, look like his own.

Stories about Eliezer's enforcement of the law are strikingly limited to household matters, involving his own practice and his disciples', on the one side, and that of his own village, on the other. Presumably Eliezer's disciples accepted his view that sometimes a long prayer is called for, other times a short one. His own son did as he said. His village is alleged to have followed his rule about circumcizing on the Sabbath. Eliezer told his disciple Ilai not to leave home on the festival. Tarfon in Lydda enforced Eliezer's rule on fasting for rain.

Other precedents or cases, when cited, do not allege Eliezer's view was enforced either by his own efforts or by those of others. They claim only that others earlier had done what Eliezer claims is supposed to be done. We therefore cannot demonstrate that Eliezer enforced the laws he taught, as either a village-authority, or an officer of a larger rabbinical government, or a Roman official. In fact the only laws, except ones on fasting and circumcision on the Sabbath, which do indicate practical enforcement pertain to the private affairs of Eliezer's family and immediate circle of disciples. At most it may be claimed that Eliezer exercised severely limited religious authority in his own town. Since the larger number of the laws which might have produced stories about enforcement pertains to agricultural, family, and cleanness law, it is striking that no evidence suggests either how such laws might have been enforced or that they actually were carried out, on Eliezer's instructions or otherwise, by ordinary folk.

That fact, however, does not suggest that the bulk of Eliezer's laws consisted of purely theoretical rulings. Apart from the Temple laws of various kinds, it seems likely that Eliezer's laws were made because people were expected to keep them. But those who would keep them would do so because they acknowledged Eliezer's authority as a learned man, not because he could either coerce or frighten people to do what he said as a government official or holy man. Who would have been expected to keep the agricultural and cleanness laws, if not loyal Pharisees, by whom Eliezer, among others, presumably was regarded as a great master of the old tradition and its disciplines and a reliable authority on new issues, practical or otherwise? The absence of precedents and case-reports therefore should suggest that the nature of the application of sectarian law was different from that of common law -- civil, criminal, and the like, or of religious law pertinent to people not part of the sect -- Sabbath, festival, and holy day rules, slaughtering and other laws, and the laws of menstrual purity. The Pharisees after 70 would have been instructed in the law as they were before then, by men whose qualification consisted not of 'official' recognition but of the consensus of the sect itself. The status of authority was conferred, therefore, within the group, by processes we cannot now describe, and not achieved by some objectively demonstrated accomplishments or imposed by institutionalized, governmental recognition or by rabbinical support.

The later rabbinical government, which formally authorized its members to effect the law in courts or local authorities, and which enjoyed official status within the Roman and Iranian regimes, seems to have had no counterpart in Eliezer's time, at least so far as he was concerned. Such authority as Eliezer may have exercised outside of his limited circle depended upon nothing more than respect for his opinions on the part of other Pharisees. We have, however, slight knowledge, if any, about where such Pharisees might have been located, how they knew about Eliezer's opinions, or why they accepted them.

vii. Eliezer's Program for Yavneh

Eliezer's program for Yavneh conforms to that already revealed in the historically reliable pericopae. In general he seems to have taken a moderate and often lenient position on the application of the Pharisaic discipline. Along with others of his time he evidently added to the former concerns the effort to define in a fairly precise way the procedures for keeping laws formerly not so carefully applied in detail. Such exact rules include the size of a field liable for Pe'ah, what to do with a field wholly consisting of defective clusters (an unlikely phenomenon), how much Heave-offering beyond the minimum requirement may be given, and similar matters. Eliezer opposed the imposition of fixed rules on the supplicatory part of the Eighteen Benedictions, which he hoped to preserve as a spontaneous expression. In Sabbath laws we find a tendency to a somewhat strict application of established rules. Some distinctions introduced by Eliezer, in regard to the ritual pool for instance, seem to have produced strict aspects for what were formerly lenient rules. Of this we can be less certain. The only important innovation in the historical picture introduced by the traditions concerns the central issue of Yavneh: relationships to the Romans and the possibilities of a new war.

viii. Eliezer and the Christians

The traditions introduce one further, curious point of contact with the Synoptics' picture of Jesus:

11. He said to [the Pharisees]: Which of you, having an ass or an ox that has fallen into a well, will not immediately pull him out on a Sabbath day?" And they could not reply to this -- Lk. 14:5-6 (Matt. 12:9-14: sheep; Mk. 3:1-6; Lk. 6:11; 13:10-17)

11. Tos. Y.T. 3:2: Eliezer says that if an animal and its offspring fall into the pit on the festival, one raises the first on condition of slaughtering it and does slaughter it, and feeds the second in its place, so that it will not die.

Joshua says one does not actually slaughter the first, and then raises the second to slaughter that one. So he is able to remove both from the pit.

In point of fact, neither Eliezer nor Joshua would approve immediately removing the animal from the pit on the festival except for the sake of slaughter, all the more so on the Sabbath, when slaughtering is not done. One maintains it there until it is permissible to remove it. Here Jesus's saying takes for granted a law quite the opposite of that attributed to the early Yavneans. I do not know what to make of the Gospels' certainty that the law does not prohibit doing what the early Yavneans take for granted is not allowed.

A second, and far more important pericope first occurs in Tos. Hul. 2:24. Eliezer was arrested because of minut. The story is in two parts. In the first, it is alleged that Eliezer was arrested because of minut but managed to hoodwink the judge by saying he will rely upon the judge. That ends the matter. The judge frees him. Nothing more is said about minut.

The point of the story is strikingly similar to that of the trial of Shila (b. Ber. 58a), in which Shila persuades the Iranian judge that he accepts his authority: "Blessed is the All-merciful who has made earthly royalty on the model of heavenly royalty and has invested you with dominion and made you lovers of justice." Forthwith the parastak frees Shila and sets him up as a judge. The stories do not use the same language and deal with quite different problems. They have in common the allegation that the rabbi is able to elude gentile justice by making the judge think the opposite of what is really the case; the rabbi speaks of heaven -- so both Tos. Hul. and b. Ber. explicitly allege -- but the judge supposes the rabbi means the gentile judge himself. The primary element of the story therefore contains a commonplace motif.

The second episode, tacked on to the first, is connected to the foregoing by the allegation that Eliezer was embarrassed at his arrest. Then Aqiba proposes that Eliezer has enjoyed something he learned from a min. Eliezer admits that was the case, and explicitly admits what is in Aqiba's question -- therefore is made to accept the Aqiban viewpoint that one should have no intercourse whatever with minim. Later versions of the story explain what Eliezer had approved in Jesus's sayings: money which may not be used for the Temple may be used for a privy for the high priest. This is consistent, in a general way, with Eliezer's opinions on the purchase of a Parah, which is not sacrificed in the Temple, by money of the same origin.

Certainly, Tos. is told in a Roman setting. Lieberman has established that fact. But despite the superficial marks of authenticity, we are unable to assess the beginnings of the account or of the allegation that Eliezer was arrested on suspicion of minut. We do not know when he died, and, unless we follow Graetz in finding in the story evidence that Domitian persecuted Christians, we cannot be sure that the story pertains to a persecution during Eliezer's own lifetime. We do not know why Eliezer should have been linked to minim. To make the point that clever rabbis can outwit stupid Roman judges, one need not have introduced the question of minut at all. So that detail should be integral to the tradition. But then the tradition itself ignores the occasion for the trial -- it is excluded from the account of the proceedings -- and stresses simply the rabbi's cleverness. Then Aqiba's insinuation is made the moral of the narrative. Eliezer merely accepts it and admits he was guilty of violating it. So part B is a story in which Aqiba is the master, Eliezer the disciple -- thus an Aqiban story alleging that the Torah requires the Jews to separate themselves from the minim. Clearly, such a story conforms to the viewpoint of the Bar Kokhban supporters. It is commonly supposed, in Bar Kokhba's times, the minim seen as Jewish-Christians made their final break with the Jews. Whether this is so cannot be said with certainty.

The tradition thus alleges Eliezer held one should have nothing whatever to do with minim. Such an allegation is entirely consistent with the view that Eliezer favored the xenophobic militarists, said gentiles cannot enter the world to come, favored war against peace, and otherwise supported the policies behind the Bar Kokhba War. Aqibans seem to stand behind this view of Eliezer. But one cannot show it was Aqiba himself who so stated with reference to Eliezer. He certainly cannot have been a min. But it seems difficult to say whether the account before us reports something which actually happened. It is the first narrative about something Eliezer has done, not merely a chriic setting for an important saying of his.

ix. Conclusion

The Eliezer of tradition is therefore portrayed by the most important authorities of the second century. Every effort seems to have been made to hand on generally consistent traditions, normally -- though not always -- developed out of, or closely related to the antecedent materials. No effort, systematic or otherwise, evidently was made either to suppress Eliezer's materials, to distort or falsify them, or to assign to them a negative value, as deriving from the House of Shammai or from a master who had been excommunicated. Neither theme so important in the period of the formation of the legends about Eliezer makes an appearance. To be sure, other important themes and subjects of the Eliezer-legend, beginning with his origins and ending with his death, likewise do not appear.

On the basis of the allegations concerning Eliezer among the best and the better traditions, as well as those just now reviewed, biography might be possible. But it would not be very interesting. Nearly the whole of what is put into Eliezer's mouth consists of details of a system which Eliezer has not created (any more than any other sage) and which he proposes to modify in trivial detail. If we may now refer back to Cox's suggestive statements about the purpose of biography, we may state flatly that attributing sayings to named authorities bears no relationship whatsoever to the biography of the authorities at hand. Whatever the purpose, it was not to create a person, a model, a characterization, even an exemplification of virtue or (in this context) of law.

Having reviewed pretty much everything Eliezer is supposed to have said and done, so far as matters had reached the framers of the literature to the end of the second century, we reach a simple conclusion. What we know about Eliezer as a person answers few questions we think important when studying individuals and their lives. What we know about Eliezer as a person nonetheless proved important and deeply consequential to the people who produced the documents as we have them. But so far as Eliezer -- a name -- stands for someone who lived and died and taught things, that is, someone who had a biography, the sources at hand take no interest in that matter. Why they thought it important to preserve sayings in the name of Eliezer -- as against Joshua or Aqiba, on the one side, or in no name at all, on the other -- we do not know. That constitutes the aspect of the problem of the attributed saying we do not consider here. Alas, it seems to me the interesting aspect. Closed off, however, is the matter important to earlier scholarship: Who was he? What did he really say? What did he do? These questions prove not only asymmetrical to the character of the evidence at hand. They also turn out to be rather dull, essentially beside the point.

CHAPTER SEVEN
THE ELIEZER OF LEGEND

i. Eliezer and the Amoraim

Legendary stories about Eliezer's life and times generally are unrelated to legal sayings. They tend to appear in the later strata of the Gemarot and in the late compilations of midrashim. Their formal and literary traits exhibit little in common with pericopae in the legal tradition. The disciplined articulation of Eliezer's legal principles and discrete opinions, in close association with Joshua's and Aqiba's, on the one side, and Ilai's and Judah's, on the other, has no counterpart in the legendary materials. The legends introduce personal and professional relationships which bear slight, if any, parallels, either external or internal, to the evidences of the legal traditions. For example, while in the legal materials Aqiba, Joshua and Eliezer are regarded as equals, in the legendary ones Aqiba is made into the disciple of Eliezer, sometimes also of Joshua, and not infrequently Joshua and Eliezer will be represented as co-disciples of Yohanan. And the relationship to Yohanan b. Zakkai figures prominently in the legendary sort of stories, even though it is virtually unknown to the legal stratum. Clearly the use of the poor traditions for biographical and historical purposes will not be easy. Yet one cannot evade the task, for the purpose of the presentation and analysis of the traditions is not entirely carried out without posing historical questions to, not only about, those traditions.

It remains to ask, Was any particular Amora, individually or as part of a circle, especially involved in the formation and development of materials about Eliezer? Only Rav Judah, through both Samuel and Rav, made a disproportionate number of references to the Eliezer-tradition. But what he contributed was the allegation that the law will be in accord with Eliezer's opinion. Otherwise only in specific and isolated pericopae do we find special interests introduced into the formulation of Eliezer-stories, i.e., Joshua b. Levi (important also in the Yohanan-tradition, at exactly the same points). Ba and Hiyya b. Ba seem to have had a good opinion of Eliezer. For the rest, the Amoraic allusions are episodic, and reveal no pronounced tendency either to favor him or to denigrate him or to treat him other than routinely, as part of the larger group of early masters.

ii. Origins, Early Life, Education

The legends do not provide Eliezer with much of a biography. They add three important stories, the origins, excommunication, and the (closely-related) death scenes. Otherwise, Eliezer tends to appear not as an individual but as part of a redactional formula, along with Joshua, or with Joshua and Aqiba.

It is difficult to show that any details in the stories of Eliezer's origins (<u>Eliezer</u> I, pp. 394-452) actually derive from his life. Eliezer and Joshua are routinely alluded to in y. Meg. 1:9 as the wonder-children who explain the mysterious meanings of the final letters. y. knows nothing about the story of Eliezer's beginning his studies as a mature man. It takes for granted that he spent his childhood with Joshua. It is difficult to see how the legends of Eliezer's origins could have been known to the authority behind the interpolation of Eliezer's and Joshua's names into a story about the wonder-children. So on the face of it the stories about Eliezer's origins ought to come after the interpolation of Eliezer's and Joshua's names in y. Meg. -- that is, late in Amoraic times, not much before the beginning of the fourth century at the earliest.

ARN, the first in the several versions, takes for granted the relationship to Yohanan, which it (obviously) has learned from M. Avot itself. But where did it get the notion that Eliezer came only after the others in the circle -- Joshua, Yosi the Priest -- had already assembled as Yohanan's disciples? Only the story-line requires it. ARN also omits reference to the name of the father-in-law, Gamaliel's father, Simeon. This is not a noteworthy omission; it is not central to ARN's account. But the chria about bad breath is important, the second major theme in the account, after the story about leaving the plough to study Torah. Then the third theme, about the disinheritance which produced the contrary action, completes the account. This is surely homiletical. Gen. R. has all three elements, but adds the subject of the homily: Gen. 14:15. Tanhuma contributes to the repertoire a substantial elaboration of the disinheritance motif. Eliezer is made the bad son, who leaves his father in time of troubles. Then comes the bad-breath chria. Then a colloquy further develops the story about the disinheritance. Finally Hyrcanus gives the son more than his brothers. Of these three stories, the first, about leaving the family to study Torah, seems to allege the most as biography. It claims factual knowledge of a specific person and is not merely a setting for a striking saying. The "bad breath" element is a chria in which the result of studies in poverty is represented as eventual fame. The disinheritance-motif, however fully developed, is nothing more than a homily in the guise of a biographical narrative; Torah not only is worth more than material wealth, but also produces great wealth from penitent parents. If the first element is historically sound, then Eliezer ought to have come from a wealthy family but to have displeased his family by adhering to Yohanan. We have very little evidence about Eliezer's own material situation; he may have had some orchards, but that does not make him a wealthy man. If he came from Lydda, on the plain, then he should not have been given a field in the mountains to plough, so that detail is probably imaginary. It is not easy to suggest what details might not be equally imaginary.

An interesting set of materials links Eliezer to Yohanan and omits reference to all the other disciples. These materials in part are merely redactional but in some cases represent Eliezer as the sole disciple and an exceptionally loyal one. Eliezer is tied to Yohanan in Sifre Deut. 144, expanded by b. Sanh. 32b to include many other masters, down to Rabbi. What is taken for granted in Sifre is that Yohanan and Eliezer are alike, and both conducted good courts. y. Ber. 2:3 joins Eliezer to Yohanan. Yohanan wore his tefillin all the time "and so did his disciple Eliezer." y. Sanh. 1:2 presents the saying of Ba, that Yohanan ordained Eliezer and Joshua; Joshua ordained Aqiba; and Eliezer is dropped. That Yohanan was the master of the two is taken for granted. None of these pericopae knows anything about the other disciples of Yohanan. Sifre Deut. may have been formulated before M. Avot. But Ba stands behind y. Sanh.; he may have drawn the correct conclusion from the absence of materials about the other disciples: they were not very important.

The stories that make Eliezer into the disciple of Yohanan then stand quite separately. They make the point that Eliezer was the loyal disciple and did everything his master did. This allegation would later be developed into the claim that he also never said anything his master had not said. Since the link between Eliezer and Yohanan is unattested before M.-Tos., it would seem to be of particular importance in the third century, at which time the contrary allegation that Eliezer was a Shammaite also was repeatedly made. This is furthermore when the Mishnah's promulgation produced the necessity to systematize the rules of deciding the law in moot cases. One rule clearly was that the law follows the House of Hillel. Another was that Eliezer was a Shammaite; therefore the law will not follow him. That point, to be sure, cannot have registered with the Rav Judah-Samuel circle, to which are attributed several rulings in favor of Eliezer's law. The contrary polemic was that Eliezer either was not a Shammaite; or that, whatever he was, he did just what his master did, and his master was Yohanan -- therefore his laws should be regarded as normative because he was a Hillelite like his master. It therefore seems likely that the allegations about Eliezer's disciplehood to Yohanan were important in post-Mishnaic times. That he actually was Yohanan's disciple is unlikely. We do not know with whom he studied, and the legends do not supply much credible evidence on that subject.

Separate from the allegation that Yohanan was Eliezer's master is the repeated claim that Eliezer always copies his master(s) -- who are not named. That claim should be prior to the one linking Eliezer to Yohanan and perhaps generated the further necessity to specify the master's name. Tos. Yev. 3 contains the earliest allegation that Eliezer's enigmatic replies were on account of his lacking traditions from his masters. It looks like an interpolated gloss, for other Tos. versions know nothing of this reason for his peculiar replies to questions. Tos. Suk. 1:9 has a story in which Eliezer gave enigmatic answers to his disciple's questions. At the end, b. Suk. 27b's baraita-version glosses: "Not in order to evade, but because he never said anything he had not heard from his master." The story in Tos. Kip. 3:14 about the rites of the penitential goat represents Eliezer as giving enigmatic answers to the several questions. b. Yoma 66b likewise glosses the story, not only adding new questions, but also alleging that he did not wish to put the disciples off, but he would not repeat a law he had not heard from his master. Consequently he would not answer their questions. The interpolation takes for granted the allegation that Eliezer never said anything other than traditions of his master(s). But it does not allude to Yohanan, as does b. Suk. 27b-28a. In b. Suk. 27b-28a, Eliezer's stay with Yohanan b. R. Ilai at Caesarea is narrated, with the moral that Eliezer did not evade the question but had never said anything he did not hear from his master. To this is adjoined a summary, with an interpolation of Yosi b. Judah. Then Eliezer is asked, "Are all your words only reproductions of what you have heard?" He replies that he never says anything he has not heard: "During all my life no man was earlier than myself in the school house. I never slept or dozed, nor did I leave anyone behind me when I left, nor did I ever utter profane speech, nor did I ever say a thing I did not hear from my teacher." Then comes Yohanan b. Zakkai, of whom it is alleged that he never uttered profane talk, never came after anyone else to the school house, never slept or dozed in the school house, never left anyone when he went out, and never said anything he had not heard from his teacher. Finally, Hillel, with the eighty disciples, of whom Yohanan was least, is attached. Eliezer is dropped. And finally comes Jonathan b. Uzziel. The complex pericope stresses, therefore, that Eliezer copied Yohanan, Yohanan copied Hillel. Thus Eliezer is the true heir of Hillel. But the redactor has made that point, which is absent in the prior materials.

Of Eliezer's personal life, the legendary stratum says little. Eliezer was firm that one does not mourn the death of a servant (y. Ber. 2:8). Gamaliel did so. Thus Eliezer was supposed to have been part of the slave holding-class, as were (other) third- and fourth-century masters. Abbahu (y. Yev. 13:2) tells the story of Eliezer's marrying the daughter of his sister at his mother's request, despite his view that such a marriage to a minor is not legal. ARN drops the attribution to Abbahu and also the reference to Eliezer's mother. The niece is given the chief part.

Two other allegations about Eliezer's education are made. First, he and Joshua showed an interest in cosmological questions. Second, they traded information on how to produce children or male children. Eliezer and Joshua debate the source of rain-water. Eliezer says it comes from the ocean, Joshua, from the waters of the firmament (b. Ta. 9b). Their dispute extended to other cosmological questions: whether the world is completely enclosed by the firmament or not (b. B.B. 25a-b); whether the world was created from the center or from the sides; and whether the world was created from separate materials -- heaven and earth -- or from the same materials (b. Yoma 54b). I see no connection to Maaseh-Bereshit-mysticism. Eliezer and Joshua discussed (b. B.B. 10b) what to do in order to produce sons. Eliezer says one should give generously to the poor. Joshua says one should be considerate of the wife's sexual desires. Later versions will have Eliezer give that advice and greatly elaborate it.

Rav Judah-Rav (b. Sanh. 17b) say Eliezer, Joshua, Aqiba, and Simeon the Temanite all could speak seventy languages. So it is alleged that his education included the study of languages. y. Meg. 1:9 has Jeremiah in Hiyya b. Ba's name say [C]Aqilas translated the Torah [=presented his translation] before Eliezer and Joshua. They approved it. b. Meg. 3a turns this into the allegation that they dictated the translation to him. On this basis S. Lieberman alleges Eliezer (and Joshua) knew Greek, for the translation was into that language, so Greek in Jewish Palestine (N.Y., 1942), pp. 16-19: "In the court of Jabneh... there were four members who spoke them [many languages].... It is possible that he [Eliezer] acquired his secular learning in his youth, while still at home.... Here [with reference to [C]Aqilas] there can be no doubt whatever that TP speaks of the Greek translation of the Bible by Aquila, who read it before R. Eliezer and R. Joshua, and was highly praised for it. This commendation can be appreciated only if the men who uttered it were qualified to pass judgment on the style and exactness of the translation. And it is obvious that the source in TP regarded them as able critics of Greek style." While it is clear that Hiyya b. Ba took for granted Eliezer knew Greek, it is difficult to find much evidence of that fact in the more reliable materials. The sayings based on Aristotelian science and cosmology do not much change the picture.

One cannot positively demonstrate that any of these folkloristic materials contains historically reliable information on Eliezer's origins, early life, and education.

iii. Eliezer's Active Career. Eliezer and Hillel

Eliezer certainly taught law to disciples. Just as it is alleged that he never taught what he had not heard, so it is claimed that disciples were prohibited from passing their opinion in his presence. This allegation is contradicted by the stories about Aqiba's numerous disputes with Eliezer, accompanied by the allegation that Aqiba was Eliezer's disciple. Sifra Shemini Mekhilta deMilu^{c}im 2:32-3 presents Eliezer's rule that a disciple must not teach the law in his master's presence. A story is also told to illustrate the same point. Eliezer further explains the death of Nadab and Abihu on account of their having taught in Moses's presence. This view does not depend upon a close exegesis of a verse. Sifra Mekhilta deMilu^{c}im = b. Sanh. 52a presents a dispute between Eliezer and Aqiba about where the sons of Aaron died. Eliezer says it was outside, Aqiba says it was within the sanctuary. This dispute does not seem closely connected to Eliezer's view of the cause of their deaths.

Aqiba reports (y. Naz. 7:1) that he studied with Eliezer and Joshua. The two masters are represented as conducting a single academy. Aqiba's studies with Eliezer and Joshua, furthermore, are routinely alluded to in b. Ned. 50a, the "rich wife, poor scholarly husband"-version of Aqiba's beginnings. y. B.Q. 4:5 has Aqiba address Eliezer as "rabbi" and say that Eliezer's Scriptural exegesis is unnecessary, for its point is obvious. b. B.Q. 41b-42a has the same story, but greatly expands it. M. B.Q. 4:5 lacks Eliezer's exegesis and attributes the law to an anonymous, general rule. b. Pes. 69a and y. Pes. 6:3 take for granted that Aqiba was Eliezer's disciple. y. Pes. says the argument in M. Pes. 6:2 took place thirteen years after Aqiba began his studies. Joshua claims Eliezer had formerly despised Aqiba and now, after thirteen years, had to take him seriously. This element must be intended to account for the several composite pericopae, in which Eliezer opposes Joshua, then Aqiba, in that order.

The two are contrasted, with Eliezer at a disadvantage; for example, Eliezer prayed for rain without success. Then Aqiba's prayer was answered. Aqiba was forebearing, and Eliezer was not, so b. Ta. 25b. We find no story of how Aqiba obeyed Eliezer's rule against teaching law in the master's presence, but a great many which implicitly, and some which explicitly, state the opposite. The illness of Eliezer (Mekh. Bahodesh 10: 58-86) is a story about Aqiba's excellent instruction. All that is important for Eliezer is that he was ill. Tarfon, Joshua, Eleazar b. ^{c}Azariah, and Aqiba then supply the important characters, with the first three setting the stage for the last and best. It is a story about Aqiba, and its point is commonplace in the Aqiban corpus, that suffering is a good thing. Eliezer is not even given a chance to praise Aqiba's saying. The structure knows nothing about Eliezer and Joshua as disciples of Yohanan. Joshua is no different from Tarfon, Aqiba and Eleazar; he calls Eliezer "my master," not "my brother." This genre of chriic settings was popular among those responsible for the midrashic compilations. The Avot-list of Yohanan's disciples, for example, generates ARN Chap. Fourteen, the story of the death of Yohanan's son, with Eliezer, Joshua, Yosi, Simeon, and Eleazar coming to pay respects. Eleazar comes at the end and is given the best saying. The same genre, not so well developed through narrative, occurs with reference to Ps. 14:34, the kindness of the peoples. But we should have further examples of the same "standard list" of disciples of Eliezer: Tarfon, Joshua, Eleazar b. ^cAzariah, and Aqiba. This is the only such "list" -- a strange anomaly.

A second important associate was Joshua. While the interpolation of their names, as wonder-working children, suggests they were together from their earliest years, other stories treat them as associates only in their active careers. Eliezer and Joshua are joined in a number of stories. In b. B.B. 74b they are on a ship. Joshua sees a light, and Eliezer says it is the eye of Leviathan. The story about Eliezer, Joshua, and the insolent widow's son (b. Qid. 31a) has Eliezer as the reasonable party, Joshua as the irritable one. In Gen. R. 70:5 Eliezer treats the proselyte, ^cAqilas, in a short-tempered way, and Joshua is patient, parallel to Shammai and Hillel in b. Shab. 30b-31a. Qoh. R. 1:8.4 has the same pattern. Eliezer and Joshua are introduced into the story (y. Hag. 2:1) of the circumcision of Elisha b. Abbuyah. They were in Jerusalem and invited to the celebration. While others caroused, they studied Torah. But their studies produced supernatural effects -- the effects like those described in the Merkavah-stories -- and so Elisha's father decided he wanted his son to have the same power. This spoiled the effect of the pious deed, and Elisha eventually went bad. So study of Torah should not be undertaken in order to attain supernatural or magical power -- a standard rabbinical piety.

Eliezer, Joshua, and Aqiba are routinely joined in connection with the Abba Judah-story (y. Hor. 3:4). They are not differentiated and play no important role in the sotry: they represent "the sages," nothing more. The story (Sifre Deut. 38) of Eliezer, Joshua, and Saddoq at Gamaliel's banquet has nothing to do with Eliezer. He serves merely to raise question to be answered by the others -- Joshua and Saddoq.

Three legal issues are well-attested for the Yavnean period, the initiation of proselytes, the date of Pentecost, and the rules on saying the Shema and the Prayer. The first clearly was debated among Jewish- and gentile-Christians; the second was a matter of sectarian debate, distinguishing Pharisees from Sadducees, and the third certainly goes back to the redactional agendum of Eliezer, Joshua, and Gamaliel. b. Yev. 46a/y. Qid. 3:12 has the dispute between Eliezer and Joshua on the initiation of proselytes. Eliezer says it is all right if the proselyte is circumcised but not baptized. Joshua says it is all right if he is baptized and not circumcised. The sages say both are required. b. Men. 65b gives Eliezer and Joshua differing proofs for the proposition that Pentecost does not have to fall on the day after the Sabbath. Eliezer's depends upon the words, For yourself (Deut. 16:9) -- just as with reference to the Sukkah and lulav Joshua says there has to be something distinctive at the commencement of the counting. Ishmael offers a different proof entirely, and Judah b. Batyra gives a heqqesh. In Sifra Vayiqra 13:4 = b. Men. 68a, Eliezer proves from a heqqesh that the omer must be barley. Aqiba provides a proof from logic.

Eliezer proves that the whole Shema does not require the heart's intention. Only the first line does. Scripture says These words -- so the foregoing will require intention ("Be upon thy heart") but not the rest. Aqiba says that the continuation, Which I command you this day on your heart means the whole passage requires intention (Midrash Tannaim to Deut. 6:6, Hoffmann, p. 26 = b. Ber. 13a). An ^cam ha'ares is one who does not read the Shema morning and evening, so Eliezer. Joshua says it is a person who does not put on tefillin, Ben Azzai says it is a person who does not have sisit on his garment (b. Ber. 47b). One should wipe with the left hand, not the right, because he eats with it. Joshua says it is because one writes with it. Aqiba says because one points with it to the accents in the Scroll (b. Ber. 62a). Such ritualization of everyday routine is a mark of rabbinism, but that does not mean the sayings cannot be authentic. Eliezer says (b. A.Z. 7b) that one asks for his own needs and then recites the Prayer. Joshua says the opposite. These opinions are tied to proof-texts (Ps. 102:1, Gen. 24:63 vs. Ps. 142:3, respectively), but the proof-texts are not integral to the argument.

The most important event in Eliezer's active career was the excommunication. y. M.Q.'s story about Eliezer's excommunication is attested by Hanina and Jeremiah. b. B.M. 59a-b reorganizes and develops y.'s primitive version. The issue is the same; the authority of Heaven in deciding the law. Eliezer is on the side of the House of Hillel, which believed in heavenly echoes, against the Shammaites, represented by Joshua, who do not. The intrusion of Nathan is curious. Aqiba occurs in both versions as the leading disciple. He is the suitable person -- and Joshua is not mentioned. Gamaliel's absence is explained: he is on a voyage. But he is subject to the supernatural wrath attendant upon the rejection of the heavenly opinion, so should have been involved. Then Imma Shalom is introduced. Her story stresses Eliezer's supernatural power. y. knows nothing about either Gamaliel or Imma Shalom. y. limits supernatural elements to the claim that the echo may decide the law. Eliezer's ability to curse and Gamaliel's tidal wave are unknown. In general, therefore, b. tends to introduce supernatural and magical elements unknown to y. and to give them an important place in the narrative. Jeremiah in y. knows only of his being able to cast an evil eye; that element does recur in b. (I), without attribution to Jeremiah. It is exceeded by the stories that accompany it. The "oven of ^cAkhnai" plays no role in the narratives. Once it is mentioned it is forgotten -- so it looks like an interpolation, for it is superfluous to the account. I cannot imagine why it has been introduced.

We have four last-illness-and-death stories. First, y. Shab.'s version of Eliezer's death-scene has only Hyrcanus, his son, and "the disciples" -- Joshua is the only one named. Joshua again appears as the sole disciple. Later on, his saying will be given to

Aqiba and expanded into a chria, with Aqiba witnessing the funeral cortege on its journey from Caesarea (not mentioned in y. Shab.) to Lydda. It is taken for granted that the disciples will come to the death-scene, but they are not given individual parts to say. They simply affirm that he is "clean." This must mean that the excommunication is in the background, and F. makes it explicit: Joshua says the "vow" has been released. b. Sanh. 68b changes everything. It first accounts for the transfer of the cucumbers/magic saying from Joshua to Eliezer. Eliezer is sick, but, clearly, a death-scene is in hand, so the parallel to Mekh./Sifre is clear. Aqiba is now the chief mourner and disciple. Joshua is subordinated but is still made to announce "the vow" is released. Once it is shown that Eliezer is lucid, it is possible to raise legal questions. These are introduced first of all to show that Eliezer has been excommunicated. So that theme, subordinated in y., becomes important in b. Aqiba is rebuked for not coming sooner. His death as a martyr is alluded to -- thus the Aqiban martyrdom stories are in hand as well. The 'decline of the generations' is now given explicit details. Eliezer learned a great deal but not all of what his masters knew, and he taught a great deal but not all of what he knew. Then comes a separate story about Eliezer's mastery of magic -- a unique pericope. The five cleanness-rules are then reaffirmed. At the end Aqiba is given the honor of delivering a eulogy.

Second, Rabbah b. b. Hana's story about Eliezer's (last) illness is strikingly different from Mekhilta's. Rabbah knows nothing of the "four disciples". All he knows is that Aqiba will say the opposite of the others. They weep. He rejoices. Eliezer is now certified as a candidate for entry into the world to come. So he is happy. But Eliezer is then told by Aqiba that he is not perfect. Rabbah's story is remarkably ignorant of the other death-scenes. We have no hint as to the excommunication, let alone the colloquies and events surrounding the death. The Babylonian last-illness-story cannot be composed by people aware of the Palestinian one(s).

b. Ber. 28b presents a third sort of death scene, following, but not closely modeled on, that of Yohanan, and redacted along with it. Eliezer gives three sayings. The scene supplies background for the sayings. Nothing happens. No illusion is made to the excommunication; no disciples are mentioned. Aqiba's priority is not alluded to.

ARN Chap. 20 comes last of all. First, b. Ber. is summarized, though the difficult saying about keeping children back from 'reasoning' is dropped. This leaves two sayings, to be careful for one another's honor and to pray with diligence. Eleazar b. ^cAzariah is now credited with the uncleanness-teachings -- a role he does not have in b. Sanh.

ARN Chap. 25 then repeats b. Sanh. The cucumbers/magic problem is omitted. It is central to b. Sanh. but irrelevant to the story, therefore represents a Babylonian embellishment generated by the problem of the confused traditions on cucumbers/magic. ARN's new version further expands the story in various details, for instance, "three hundred laws about the bright spot," and the litany about how much Eliezer had learned and how little he taught. Eleazar b. ^cAzariah is introduced as the first mourner.

A fourth sort of death-scene (y. Sot. 9:16) is produced by Jacob b. R. Idi-Joshua b. Levi. Now two scenes are explicitly modeled on one another -- Eliezer's on Yohanan's. Yohanan says Hezekiah is coming; Eliezer says Yohanan is coming. Both take account of the cleanness-considerations attendant upon the momentary presence of a corpse (their own) in the courtyard. This composite is joined to still another. First, it is announced that "the elders" are told Hillel is worthy of the holy spirit, and Samuel is also worthy. Then the story is expanded to include Eliezer. So Eliezer is represented by Jacob-Joshua as the third in line from Hillel, the worthy disciple. y. A.Z. rearranges the pericopae but does not change the picture. Clearly, Joshua b. Levi is responsible for the stories linking Eliezer to Hillel. Yohanan is not mentioned, but Joshua has other stories about him. And Yohanan's death-scene is attached, so he cannot be out of mind in the second story. There can be no doubt that, so far as Joshua b. Levi is concerned, Eliezer is a Hillelite -- and one of the most important to them. He knows nothing of Eliezer's having been excommunicated. That element, central to b. Sanh. and alluded to y. Shab., plays no role at all.

Of the legendary allegations concerning Eliezer's active career, most may be taken as fact. He certainly taught disciples. Ilai is the only one clearly a disciple in the earliest strata of the tradition. Aqiba probably was not a disciple; the predominance of his redactors in the formation of composite pericopae seems ample evidence that he was an equal, not a subordinated, master. I see no reason to suppose Tarfon, Eleazar b. ^cAzariah, and Joshua were Eliezer's students. Tarfon may have had some sort of close association. Eleazar and Joshua were independent masters. Gamaliel is underrepresented in the legends. He should have a more important role, considering his position at Yavneh. He is left out where he clearly belongs, in the excommunication story, only in the later developments being introduced chiefly on account of supernatural considerations, and then because of his sister. The legal issues connected with Eliezer's active career all look genuine, though we cannot take for granted Eliezer's particular part in settling them. The date of Pentecost required numerous masters' proofs, Eliezer among them. The Shema certainly was an important Yavnean problem; Eliezer's opinion may be genuine. The discussion on when to say a prayer for one's own needs contradicits Eliezer's better-attested opinion that one should not have a fixed text for the Prayer to begin with, therefore is spurious.

The stories about Eliezer's excommunication and death are closely linked. One death-scene takes for granted the excommunication story and should be regarded as part of the same picture. It then is to be linked to the masters who give evidence of knowing it -- but not of having told it: Jeremiah, Hanina. So it was a Palestinian story, known in, and developed by, Babylonian circles. What lies behind it is difficult to say. It was in the third century that the acceptability of Eliezer's legal rulings was much discussed; then he was called a Shammaite; it was alleged that the Tannas do not carefully transmit his teachings; and in other ways it was made clear that one does not rely upon laws in his name. Then how to account for the inclusion of his many pericopae? The reason is that at the end he was released from the ban.

But what to begin with produced a story of a debate on heavenly intervention and the rule of the majority, ending in Eliezer's excommunication? Here only the most tentative speculation seems possible. First, in the background of every debate on heavenly intervention must lie the allegation that Hillel would have received the holy spirit had the generation been worthy of it, so anyone in the rabbinical movement who enjoys heavenly support should be represented as a follower of Hillel. This, indeed, is made clear by the Shammaite rejection of the heavenly testimony.

Now, that Eliezer is linked to Hillel is one of the fundamental implicit assertions of the legendary materials. This point has already been made clear in both legal traditions and aggadic sayings. For example, Eliezer's saying that one should not worry about the morrow (b. Sot. 48b) makes him a disciple of Hillel, who said the same thing. Shammai said something different. Mekhilta deR. Simeon b. Yohai then develops the idea into a dispute with Joshua, who agrees with the Shammaites, The heqqesh-argument (bringing is said with reference to the omer [Lev. 23:10] and to the showbreads [Lev. 23:17]) is attributed to Eliezer in b. Shab. 131a. Hillel's argument based on the heqqesh drawn from In its season is attributed to Eliezer in M. Pes. 6:2-3. But the relation to Hillel is explicit as well, for Eliezer's master now is Yohanan. He always did as his master did, said only what his master said. One set of death-stories stresses this very point. Eliezer's death was modeled after Yohanan's. And in that same pericope is the story of Hillel's being worthy of the holy spirit, and of Eliezer's like merit. So every important exemplum of the Eliezer-Yohanan connection will contain allegations about the further connection to Hillel. Palestinian masters, Jacob b. R. Idi-Joshua b. Levi stand behind these allegations.

Receiving the holy spirit, moreover, now is set against the will of the majority of the sages. So one must ask, Of whom is it alleged both that he had supernatural power and that he also had the power to subvert the will of the majority? One obvious candidate is Judah the Patriarch -- of his heirs we can presently say nothing -- who both was regarded as on the Messianic seed and claimed descent from the Messiah through Hillel. Elijah used to come to his academy (b. B.M. 85b); when Rabbi lay dying, he had knowledge of what was happening in distant places (b. Qid. 72a); he was called the Messiah (y. Shab. 16:1, b. Sanh. 98b); he had the power to cause a tooth-ache for Hiyya (b. B.M. 85b); he was as great as Moses (b. Git. 59a, b. Sanh. 36a). Clearly, Rabbi was portrayed as a supernatural figure, not exactly as was Hillel and Eliezer in respect to the Holy Spirit, but in other important ways as having been more than an ordinary sage.

One way of opposing the patriarchal preeminence was to assert that supernatural authority carries no weight against the consensus of the sages. The story about Eliezer stresses that very point. To be sure, Gamaliel is inserted into the story of Eliezer's excommunication. But he is not integral to the story; his name is introduced only later on in its development; and he plays no important role. The story represents Joshua as the leader of those who deny supernatural authority in the formation of the law; Joshua likewise is represented as the leader of those who threw out Gamaliel for his high-handedness. In all, the patriarchal authority, which rests upon the claim of descent from Hillel and thence to the Messiah, stands over against the right of the majority of the sages, led by Joshua, to make decisions. In that context the story of Eliezer's excommunication ought to have been generated. And it strikingly accords with sayings attributed to Rabbi about Eliezer's authority -- "I would decide the law in accordance with his opinion, but the Tannas do not accurately portray his opinion."

While the excommunication is important to the death-scene involving the declaration that the ban has been lifted, it plays no role in the others, which know nothing about a ban or the need to release it. Rabbah b. b. Hana's story is simply a chria for two sayings of Aqiba, first, that Eliezer is suffering now but will enjoy the next world, second that Eliezer was not perfect -- both routine sentiments. b. Ber.'s version of Eliezer's death ties Eliezer to Yohanan, but the death-scene provides merely a dramatic setting for some wise sayings on Eliezer's part. Joshua b. Levi's scene also links Eliezer to Yohanan, but the relationship now is integral, and produces not only the same last words -- no clean (as with Aqiba the martyr) but prepare a throne, but also a further allegation about Eliezer as the continuator of Yohanan-Hillel. Whether Joshua b. Levi's stories form a part of a larger case in behalf of a patriarchate, which alleged itself to enjoy access to supernatural counsel, we cannot yet determine. The story of the excommunication plays no part in Joshua b. Levi's sayings, so the stemma may be entirely separate from the excommunication + death sequence involving Aqiba, Joshua, and Eleazar b. ^{C}Azariah.

That any of these materials goes back to events in Eliezer's own life seems to me unlikely. They all form part of the third-century rabbis' efforts to supply the first and early second century authorities with biographies. But the biographies manifestly ignore the personal traits of the individuals under discussion and focus upon either homiletical or political themes pertinent to the third-century rabbinical estate, on the one side, or to the patriarchal-rabbinical institution, on the other.

iv. Eliezer's Historical Situation

The destruction of the Temple figures more prominently in the legends than in the historical and traditional materials. To be sure, Eliezer's egress from Jerusalem -- if he was there before 70 -- is not the subject on an individual story. Eliezer's and Joshua's part in Yohanan's escape consists in serving as names for the disciples who carried the bier, so b. Git. 56a and all other, and later versions. The two disciples play no important part in the story, which simply takes for granted that they were the chief assistants and ignores the other members of Yohanan's Avot-circle.

The saying of Eliezer the Great (M. Sot. 9:15) relates the decline of the generations to the destruction of the Temple. The redactional framework involves nearly the whole of the Tannaitic movement, but omits Eliezer; the close relationship to the saying of Pinhas b. Yair is to be noted (Vol. I, p. 394). The saying produces a commonplace sentiment about the destruction of the Temple. Eliezer regretted it, along with everyone else. But is is not for that reason to be regarded as not genuine. Eliezer is given a number of similar sayings in quite unrelated materials; he stresses the inevitable loss of learning, though this is not tied to the destruction of the Temple. In all, he may well have regarded the decline of the generations as a trait of times. If he did, he was wrong, for Yavnean times were marked by noteworthy creative achievements, in which Eliezer himself took an active part.

Eliezer occurs in the colloquy of Yohanan and the disciples on the meaning of Prov. 14:34 (b. B.B. 10b). All agree that the peoples are incapable of doing real kindness (hesed). Such a sentiment is congruent to the xenophobic stratum of Eliezer's materials, but not to the historically more reliable assertions about relationships to gentiles, Samaritans, and non-Pharisees.

Mid. Tan. to Deut. 14:22, Hoffmann ed. pp. 77-8, gives Eliezer and Ishmael the "rabbinical" sentiment that the Temple was a place where Torah was studied and service to the Temple led to the study of Torah -- so was subordinated to it. This is the most important rabbinical sentiment attributed to Eliezer and is very likely to be spurious. Nothing in Eliezer's salvific message (below) stresses study of Torah and practicing the commandments exactly as rabbis do; only the reference in Mekh. to Moses's hands at the battle with Amalek comes close to such a rabbinical notion. One does not have to be a rabbi to say Israel will prosper by loyalty to Torah; this was the message of Deuteronomy. But one had to be a rabbi to say that the Temple was important because Torah was studied there. I doubt Eliezer, whose piety was shaped by the cultic purity laws and by the priestly claims on the produce of the holy land, said any such thing.

The major theological issues of Yavnean times -- the nature, meaning, and permanence of the covenant, the means of atonement and the scheme of redemption -- all figure prominently in the legendary materials. These issues were made urgent by the destruction. Did the end of the cult signify the dissolution of the ancient covenant between God and Israel. Others asserted just that. What was to be the sign of the covenant in the period in which the Temple lay in ruins? Eliezer is made to say that tefillin, or the Sabbath, or circumcision will now represent the covenant. Eliezer the Great (b. Ber. 6a) says that the tefillin represent the sign of God's preference for Israel. The covenant referred to in Ex. 19:5 is variously interpreted by Eliezer. Mekh. Bahodesh 2:43-5 says Eliezer holds the reference is to the Sabbath: Aqiba, to [not practicing] idolatry. Mekh. deR. Simeon, p. 41 has Eliezer refer to Passover, Aqiba to tefillin; Pesiqta Rabbati says Eliezer told ᶜAqilas that the covenant is the Sabbath and circumcision; Mekhilta deR. Simeon, p. 139, had Eliezer say the covenant is circumcision; Aqiba refers to the Sabbath, and sages now say it is not to practice idolatry. The value of circumcision and the Sabbath is further stressed by Eliezer in his interpretation of Qoh. 11:2 (b. Eruv. 40b). Joshua says the reference is to Passover and Sukkot.

Deut. 4:6 is interpreted by Eliezer to mean that a person who loves his body more than his money and one who loves his money more than his body both must love God with all they have (Sifre Deut. 32, b. Ber. 61b). Aqiba says the Scripture refers to love, even to the sacrifice of one's life, or martyrdom. Martyrdom plays no role in any saying attributed to Eliezer.

The nature of atonement and the course of the redemptive process constitute important parts in the response to the destruction. Eliezer's position emerges from a number of discrete sayings, none of which on the face of it is irrelevant to his situation. First, Eliezer says that God testifies against or warns Israel and then punishes them. Joshua says that the possibilities of further disaster are endless (Sifra Behuqotai Pereq

5:1). God's justice could destroy even the best man: Abraham, Isaac, and Jacob could not stand in judgment (b. Ar. 17a).

Eliezer and Joshua, second, discuss the forgiveness of sins, for example, y. Shab. 9:3, on the meaning of Is. 1:18. Both say that however long-standing are the sins, they can be whitened. y. Ta. 1:1 presents the dispute on the precondition of redemption. Eliezer says if the Israelites do not repent, they will not be redeemed. Joshua challenges this opinion. Then Eliezer says God will raise up a harsh king who will move the people to penitence, so it is inevitable that they will repent. b. Sanh. 97bff. changes this picture. Now Joshua says the harsh king will move the people to penitence -- so he is made to agree with Eliezer that penitence is the precondition of redemption, but the process of redemption will begin with God's moving the people to penitence. The best rendition of the dispute is Tanhuma Behuqotai 5, which has Eliezer say simply that if the Israelites repent they will be redeemed. Joshua says whether or not they repent, they will be redeemed at the inevitable end.

Eliezer, third, praises the faith of Israel at the sea, as do Shemaiah and Abtalion (Phar. I, p. 142), so Mekhilta deR. Simeon. Mekh. Bahodesh 4:36ff. has Eliezer emphasize the submission of Israel to the divine will. God spoke to them only after they had accepted what he would say. Aqiba takes for granted that this was so and interprets Ex. 19:19 to mean that God served to strengthen Moses's voice so that everyone heard just what Moses heard. Joshua says Israel in the wilderness made one journey at Moses's command, the rest at God's. Eliezer says all journeys were at God's command (Mekh. Vayassa 1:1ff.). At the redemption from Egypt God tried to tire the people out in order to test and refine them. Joshua says he showered beneficence upon them, giving them the Torah, manna, and doing miracles (Mekh. Beshallah 1:57ff.). Eliezer, however, also says the Israelites brought an idol with them when they passed through the sea (y. Suk. 4:3). Aqiba says the verse to which Eliezer refers (II Sam. 7:23) means the Israelites redeemed themselves. Eliezer says the reason the people believed in God was that he met their needs. Joshua says it was God's omnipotence which persuaded the people (Mekh. Vayassa 7:68ff.). This saying is congruent to Eliezer's contempt for those who are anxious about their material needs.

Fourth, Eliezer and Joshua argue about how the angel smote the Egyptians (b. Sanh. 95b). Eliezer says it was with his hand, Joshua says with his finger. Joshua corresponds to Yosi in Mekhilta, and Eliezer corresponds to Aqiba. The Eliezer in Mekhilta has no counterpart. But Mid. Ps. 78:15 has Eliezer as b. Sanh.'s Joshua; God smote the Egyptians with his finger. Mekh. Beshallah 7:109ff. presents the opinions of Yosi, Eliezer, and Aqiba on how many times the Egyptians were smitten in Egypt and at the sea.

Moses's war against Amalek is the theme of a set of Scriptural comments. Joshua says that Moses treated the Amalekites with a measure of mercy. Eliezer says the war against Amalek was at the divine command (Mekh. Amalek 1:173ff.). Presumably any new war must await a divine command. God took an oath that nothing would remain of the people of Amalek (Midrash on Psalms 9:10). Lam. R. gives this opinion to Joshua and has Eliezer explain that the destruction of Amalek will result in the coming of the Messiah and the final victory of monotheism (Lam. R. 3:66:9). Amalek came with defiance and not secretly (Mekh. Amalek 1:9ff.). The gesture of Moses in the battle meant that when Israel is strong in the words of Torah, to be given through Moses's hands, it would prevail, and otherwise it would not (Mekh. Amalek 1:131ff., Mekh. deR. Simeon b. Yohai, p. 121, 1s. 15-17). Rephidim was a real place. So too was Shittim (Num. 25:1). The former concerns the story of Amalek, the latter, of the Moabites (b. Bekh. 5b, b. Sanh. 106a).

Fifth, the preconditions for redemption figure in Mekh. deR. Simeon, p. 1. Eliezer says that when Israel is at its lowest point, God will descend and redeem them. Joshua interprets the descent to the bush differently, but his point is not greatly at variance. The inevitability of redemption is stressed by Eliezer with reference to Ps. 139:16. No foreordained event has failed to take place on its appropriate day. Joshua agrees (Tanhuma Bereshit 28, Pesiqta Rabbati 23:1). Both therefore hold redemption is inevitable, but, as noted, depends upon Israel's repentence. Joshua says that the redemption took place in Nisan and in the future will take place in Nisan. Eliezer says the future redemption will take place in Tishri (Mekh. Pisha 14:113-117; b. R.H. 10b and seq.). Creation took place in Tishri, according to Eliezer, and in Nisan, according to Joshua. The issue then extends to when the natural cycle of nature begins. Eliezer says it is in Tishri, Joshua, in Nisan. The same issue pertains to the birth of the patriarchs -- therefore the beginning of the people of Israel.

If we may now compose a picture of Eliezer's message in the aftermath of the destruction, it will appear something like this:

"Israel prospers when it does the will of God and suffers when it does not. Punishment is preceded by appropriate warnings. But God cannot deal with Israel solely according to the requirements of justice. Even the patriarchs could not have emerged guiltless. God has to forgive sins, and his mercy is without limit. There is, therefore, hope for the generation that has undergone punishment.

"But the generation must, nonetheless, do appropriate penance. (Joshua, who claims that grace does not depend upon atonement, is made to agree, for part of divine grace is the imposition of suffering which leads to penitence.) Another element in the penitential process is faith, which marked the redemption from Egypt and will therefore be required once more. Israel's atonement will include replication of the faith of the people at the sea and in their journeys through the wilderness.

"Just as in that time God tried the people in order to refine them, so now there will be trials and troubles. Just as now there are those who lack faith, so then there were Israelites who brought idolatry out of Egypt with them and whose faith depended upon material considerations.

"God punishes the oppressors of Israel. The Egyptians were smitten in times of old. The war against Amalek provides a model of divine support for Israel's cause. Just as nothing will remain of the memory of Amalek, so nothing will remain of the new oppressor. (The Amalek-story is given a rabbinical twist: Israel's victory depends upon Torah. But that theme is not central to the exegetical treatment of Amalek-story.)

"When will the redemption come? It will be when Israel is at its lowest point. But it is inevitable. Just as every foreordained event in Israel's history took place at its appointed time, so will the last and greatest triumph surely come. One may even posit the date of redemption. It will be in Tishri and so, corresponding to the natural order, will conclude the story of creation and the history of the children of the patriarchs, rather than (as Joshua claims) in Nisan, as a counterpart to the Exodus."

Eliezer's message therefore stresses four main themes: punishment and suffering, sin and atonement, the ultimate bad end for the oppressors, and the inevitability of redemption. One important theme is remarkable for its absence, and that is the Messianic expectation. Eliezer had no messianic sayings. The composite of his sayings about the age and its destiny leaves no room for a Messiah, a Messianic war, or a Messianic general. The generalized expectation of inevitable redemption does not produce a particular allegation that redemption is near at hand or that what is needed is merely a little patience. On the contrary, central to Eliezer's salvific story is Israel's own repentence. Upon repentence all things depend. So Israel can do something to extricate itself from it present state. But what it can do is not to make war, but rather, to repent and return to God. This viewpoint is very reliably attributed to Yohanan b. Zakkai. The Eliezer who stressed irenic relationships to the gentiles and had nothing to say about making war against Rome or laying claim to vast lands outside of Jewish Palestine also ought to be the Eliezer who stressed that the true struggle for redemption lay within the soul of Israel itself. The theological sayings pertinent to the aftermath of the destruction are not only in theme appropriate, but also in substance precisely what should have accompanied the best attested legal sayings of Eliezer about the dominant question of the day: the disaster and Israel's place in the world-empire of Rome.

We find ourselves, therefore, in the position of Judah b. Batyra (M. Neg. 9:3, 11:7). Our conclusion is that Eliezer really did carry on the tradition of his master. And in substance, if not in fact, his master really was Yohanan b. Zakkai. What Yohanan said about the situation of 70 is what Eliezer is likely to have said in later years. The message of both was that all depends not upon a Messianic war but upon Israel's own repentence and fulfillment of the requirements of the Torah. Nothing in Eliezer's message goes beyond what had already been stated by Yohanan. Nothing in Yohanan's message has been omitted. And behind Eliezer and Yohanan stands Hillel, whose affect upon Pharisaism was to turn a political party capable of partisan hatred into an irenic table-fellowship sect, with the Temple and the priesthood as the model of tis piety. The path from Hillel through Yohanan to Eliezer may, therefore, have been discovered only in much later times. But the late-second-century and third-century masters who posited such a single, straight line from Eliezer to Yohanan to Hillel -- for reasons pertinent to their own politics, to be sure, for it was in the patriarch's interest to avoid talk of Messianic wars and a fast-approaching end of time -- from our perspective were absolutely right.

CONCLUSION

The attributed saying in the earlier texts -- the Mishnah, the Tosefta, and in legal contexts in the two Talmuds -- exhibits traits that point to rules governing attributions. It was, for example, rare for sayings first appearing in later collections to attribute to an early authority opinions contradicting sayings first appearing in earlier collections. Even the program of themes on which a named authority is supposed to have commented remains fairly stable.

The attributed saying in later texts -- the compilations of exegeses of Scripture, the non-legal contexts in the two Talmuds -- may obey rules too. But it is difficult to know what those rules might have been, and it is impossible to relate the materials of the later texts to those of the earlier ones. This is in two aspects. First, stories about named masters are rare in the earlier compilations and in the legal segment of later ones. They are commonplace in the later and non-legal collections. Slight effort appears to have gone into relating these tales and narratives, on the one side, to legal principles or moral opinions, on the other. Second, and still more frustrating, exegeses of Scripture in later compilations and in non-legal ones rarely relate to anything we can find in earlier and legal compositions.

So the attributed sayings in the name of a single individual fall into three groups: legal, biographical, and exegetical. The three groups stand essentially autonomous of one another, though occasionally they intersect, thanks to the intervention of a glossator or editor. The legal sayings do seem to wish to preserve a uniformity of viewpoint or principle, so far as that can be demonstrated. The biographical units of discourse and the exegetical sayings on verses of Scripture presently appear random and episodic.

The problem of the unattributed saying turned out to have been overstated. Not much in the Mishnah stands outside of all attributions, if not because a name is attached, then because a principle associated with a named authority may appear, also, in an unattributed saying. Furthermore, the unattributed sayings rarely bear substantial and important components of the ideational structure of a Mishnah-tractate; only tractate Zabim rests upon a deep layer of ideas expressed, in the tractate itself, in sayings lacking all attributive traits. Finally, unattributed sayings pose no intractable problems in the analysis of the history of the ideas of the document in which they occur -- the Mishnah -- because what lacks attribution in no points us toward some prior layer of thought, some pre-Mishnaic fundament of reflection, now contained and preserved only in one type of saying and not in some other, in the unattributed but not in the attributed saying.

The problem of the attributed saying, by contrast, cannot be overstated. It confronts us on every page of every document of the canon of Rabbinic or Talmudic Judaism. Composers of units of discourse, compositors of collections of units of discourse, and redactors of entire documents everywhere assign sayings to named authorities, tell stories about named authorities, attribute exegeses of Scripture to named authorities. Yet we have been unable to identify principles by which they will have chosen one name (Eliezer's) in preference to some other. We do not even know why they thought it important to use names at all. We also do not know whether by using a name in a given document, the framers of that document intended us to draw one sort of conclusion, while by using a name in another document, the redactors of that other document meant to convey a different message entirely.

We therefore cannot state the intention behind either using a name or not using one. We thus do not know why the rabbinic literature bears the profoundly contradictory traits it does. That is to say, why should the documents always speak for the community as a whole, thus obliterating all marks of individual authorship, while at the same time the same documents attribute so vast a proportion of their contents to named individuals? If the literature was meant to be collective and public, a statement of the consensus of the whole, then why refer sayings to individuals at all? Why tell stories (other than to exemplify traits meant for all to copy) about named and well-known persons? Why impute to the authority of a given individual a distinctive view about a verse of Scripture? But if the literature was meant to preserve the genius of the individual, the viewpoint of the hero, then why not allow individuals to sign their names to books? And why not compose books associated with individual names?

We know, as a matter of fact, that named tradents did affix their names to their work, and their work covers vast stretches of the Talmud of Babylonia, and, to lesser measure, of the Land of Israel as well. Yet the work of the named tradent is always secondary to the content of what the tradent put together. What Yohanan says (in the early pages of Bavli Berakhot), for instance, in the name of Yose or Simeon b. Yohai is what Yose or Simeon is supposed to have said, nothing more. But, in any event, what Yohanan did was not to compose a book, or even the large part of a book, about Yose or Simeon, but only a sizable composite of what would be used, on the volition of we know not whom, in a different sort of writing and for a different purpose altogether.

Now it may be argued that the reason sayings bear names is that the person to whom a saying is attributed really did say it. Perhaps so. It remains to be demonstrated, not merely alleged. But what difference does that allegation make (if it could be shown to be true by the clean criterion of K.R. Walters, cited in the opening lines)? The questions just now presented in catalogues stand quite securely. For the issue is the character of the literature, not the validity of the allegations contained within that literature. And the question to be faced is why, in the rabbinic canon of late antiquity, named sayings occur, and why, even though they occur, they do not seem to matter much in the categorical framing of the writings. That question proves urgent, whether or not we concede people really said what other people said they said. The real problem of the attributed saying, no less than of the unattributed saying, confronts us not within the category of biography, but within the context of culture. Exactly what sort of people would write this way, and not in some other way, about these things, not other things? When we know the answer to that question, we shall also frame a suggestive theory about why, within that larger cultural aspiration, they thought it important to preserve distinctions among sayings (this saying was said by X, that saying was said by Y, and the other saying was attached to no one's name at all) that, in the end, did not make a whole lot of difference.

So the problem of the attributed saying points us toward not historical but anthropological issues: what sort of community, what sort of world-view and way of life? And the anthropological issues demand, as a first step, that we pay a call upon whatever of the community at hand we can visit, which is to say, upon the documents as such. For all that is left is the literature, each document to be read both by itself and in the context of that library of which it is an integral part, I mean, the library that is the Judaism of the rabbis of late antiquity. In that library, the books really are different from one another, even though, as we have seen, the named sayings are not. So let us continue our search, now along the right path: not into the components (the contents) of the books, the sayings whether named or not named, unattributed or attributed, but into the books themselves.